GEORGE S. FICHTER

Illustrated by

ARTHUR B. SINGER

 GOLDEN PRESS · NEW YORK
Western Publishing Company, Inc.
Racine, Wisconsin

FOREWORD

An ordinary gray cat taught me to like cats. Until then, I had accepted them only as animals that other people kept as pets.

For seven years this cat was silent. Often we studied each other intently but without rendering judgment. All the while, the cat maintained great reserve, perhaps sensing that she was in a household that had bordered being anti-cat. But with her quiet grace, she won her way. I found myself becoming an admirer not only of this particular cat but also of all her kind as the clever, calculating creatures that they are.

Time softened the gray cat, too. Now she communicates with quiet mews that get her messages to me. She has analyzed me until she knows exactly how to produce the performance that she wants. I respond to her demands with almost slavish willingness.

This cat, now part of my life for slightly over a decade, observed the writing of this entire book. When I found pad marks on the manuscript pile in the morning, I knew she had gone over the night's work with inquisitive stares and sniffs. I have no idea whether she approved, but I do hope you find this book meaningful and useful. I do regret that the cat did not get to see earlier the superb illustrations by Arthur Singer. These she will share with you.

G. S. F.

CONTENTS

THE CAT

To those who love cats—the ailurophiles—the cat is a playful, clever, courageous animal, soft, gentle, and intelligent. At the opposite extreme, and with feelings equally intense, are those who dislike the cat and who may even suffer from a morbid fear of them, a rare and unfortunate malady known as ailurophobia. But anyone who has even read this far has already declared himself to be a "cat" person. Already he has been caught up by the cat's quiet, captivating personality.

Such a creature as "the cat" truly does not exist. Each individual cat has a personality that is quite distinct from that of any of its breed or, for that matter, of its litter. Personalities of dogs, in contrast, are much more uniform within the breed.

Over a period of time of living with a cat, a master learns to know his pet's idiosyncrasies. The cat, in turn, learns its master. But the meeting place must at least be halfway—or a little in the cat's favor. A cat thrives on affection but spends little of its energy to indulge its master, while a dog makes a special effort to please his master. A cat never gives in totally. It refuses to be conquered to the extent of becoming a domestic slave. Always it holds a bit of itself in reserve.

At times a pet cat seems almost human in its understanding of how to achieve its desires. It employs its instinctive mastery of practical psychology to win its way. Ordinarily a cat will go out of its way to keep from acknowledging its dependency on you for its comforts and its well-being, but there are gratifying occasions when its affection spills over and is expressed with purring and by an insistence on being close. It is these times and moods that, for many pet owners, are most cherished.

Kittens are soft and cuddly, filled with an inquisitive playfulness and warm affection. Sometimes even an old cat reverts to kittenish ways, much to the astonishment and delight of its owner.

A mature cat displays almost regal dignity. Some become much more indifferent than others. They may be haughty or even a bit snobbish, but one need almost always breaks the barrier: a good meal that is to their liking.

THE PARADOXICAL WORLDS OF THE CAT show clearly when you open the door and let your pet out into the night. It becomes an entirely different animal, its eyes no longer soft and understanding but instead ablaze with wildness. It travels in the world of its wild ancestors, inhabited today by its untamed cousins. These include the Lion, king of beasts, and others less regal.

As wild as it may be deep inside, the domestic cat responds to affection. Though equipped with sharp fangs and hooked claws and with the ability to use them effectively, the domestic cat enjoys kindness and caresses. It does not delight in the kind of roughhouse play that please dogs and seems to be more sensitive to harsh words. Yet a cat brims with primal pride and can never relinquish its sense of basic freedom. This dual, paradoxical nature is what makes a cat so mysteriously different from other pets.

In the night, the docile house cat becomes a sly, sinewy hunter.

A cat uses its paws like hands to open doors or drawers.

CATS CAN BE CLEVER, though most commonly they refuse to do what you ask them to—at least at the time you ask it. If you try to teach your cat to open a door, you may give up in despair and conclude that the cat—yours, at least—has no intelligence. But your cat is probably just being stubborn. If on its own your cat wants to show you that it knows that the knob is the mechanism that operates the door, it will demonstrate its understanding of how it works. Cats reserve the right to use their intelligence as they see fit, which almost invariably is to benefit themselves. If you derive pleasure or benefit, too, it is coincidental.

One point is clear, however: if once you become fascinated by cats, you have acquired a lifelong occupation, for study them as well as you may, you can never part the mystic shroud that cats keep between themselves and their human masters. Cats can be loved, but they can never be totally understood.

THE CAT'S FAMILY

From the tabby to the Lion, all cats share features that make them members of a distinctive family of mammals, the Felidae. Generally, cats are divided into three groups: small cats, which can purr—a sound produced by vibrating the vocal cords; large cats, which can roar but cannot purr; and the Cheetah, the least catlike member of the family.

Typically, cats have a round, almost owlish head with big eyes that are directed forward. This is the face of a night hunter. Most cats do prowl at night, and during the day they nap. They usually creep up on their prey and then pounce rather than running to catch it. There are exceptions, of course. The most divergent is the Cheetah, which depends almost wholly on its speed to overtake its prey.

Cats walk on their toes, which have thick pads that enable them to move quietly. They have five toes on their front feet and four on their hind feet. Nearly all cats are good climbers—that is, they can go up a tree easily. Coming down is more difficult for them because, unlike squirrels, they are not able to spread their hind legs and reverse the direction of their feet so that their claws can be used to hold them in place.

Except for the Bobcat and the Lynx, the wild cats all have rather long tails. Their fur varies in length—short in those that live in warm climates, long in those that must endure cold. The pattern differs even within a species. Both the Jaguar and the Leopard, for example, occur in black phases as well as in spotted forms. The basic pattern that is most prevalent throughout the family is a dark striping on a lighter background, as in the Tiger or in tabbies.

The face of a master night hunter—large, owlish eyes directed forward, the cups of the ears turned to pick up the slightest sound.

Cats are generally solitary animals. A few kinds hunt or travel in small groups, but they are not social animals in the sense that wolves, hyenas, and other members of the dog family are.

The most distinctive features of the cats are their eyes, tongues, teeth, ears, claws, and whiskers. These are the tools with which they get their food, avoid danger, fight their battles, and keep aware of the world around them. These special parts of their anatomy are described in greater detail on the following pages.

TEETH in cats are not developed for chewing. All cats have 30 teeth—16 in the upper jaw and 14 in the lower. Even the smallest teeth are pointed and are used mainly for seizing and holding prey. In both the upper and lower jaws, the canine teeth are large and dagger-like. The jaws themselves are powerful, enabling the cats to hold their prey in an unrelenting grip.

Unable to chew, cats swallow their food in chunks. In compensation, their digestive juices are very strong so that the large pieces of food are easily assimilated. In nature, cats are almost totally meat eaters.

A CAT'S TONGUE is rough, covered with tiny, hard points. In the large cats, these are stiff enough to tear the flesh and bring blood if the cat licks you. Cats can use this rough tongue to rasp flesh from the bones of the animals they kill. These horny projections are actually modified taste buds.

A cat uses the projections on its tongue to help keep its coat clean. All cats are fastidious creatures, spending a good share of their time cleaning and adjusting their fur. The rough tongue serves as a brush or a comb to put the hair back in order when it becomes ruffled.

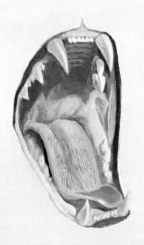
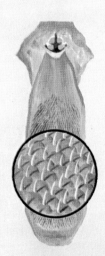

THE EYES of cats are the largest of all carnivores. Further, the size of the pupils is adjustable from mere slits in bright light to full orbs at night. At night, the cat can let in all the light that is available so that it can see when it is literally too dark for other animals to see.

A special membrane at the back of each eye reflects the light and amplifies it so that even dim light is utilized fully. It is this lining at the back of the eyes that makes a cat's eyes glow when a light is shined on them at night. If the light continues to strike the eyes, the pupils are closed down and the glow stops.

A CAT'S EARS are large, their cuplike bases extending over about half of the head. They serve as funnels to collect even the smallest sounds. Inside the ears are long, stiff hairs that act as sensors in picking up sounds. Even when a cat has its eyes closed and is apparently sound asleep, its ears may turn and twist continually to pick up and interpret the sounds in its surroundings.

No one really knows whether the cat can determine precise locations by sound, but it is certain that sounds are important guides to these night hunters in helping them locate their prey.

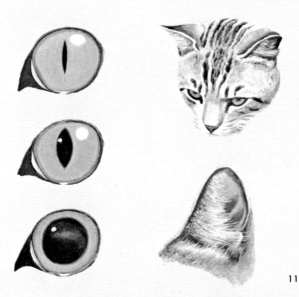

A CAT'S CLAWS are valuable tools used for climbing and also for protection and for catching prey. In all except the Cheetah, the claws can be retracted or extended. Small muscles hold them in concealment, but when the cat needs them, they can be let down—sharp and ready for action. A dog's claws cannot be retracted.

Kittens soon learn to hold in their claws when playing with people, but if a kitten or full-grown cat becomes angry, it can unleash ten curved, razor-sharp claws that can send any intruder howling. Cats scratch on trees or posts to wear down their claws, which continue to grow. The process is like filing their nails.

WHISKERS are a cat's feelers. They stick out over the cat's eyes and at the sides of its face and are highly sensitive to touch. When a cat moves through the darkness, its whiskers serve as the gauges to determine whether a space is large enough for it to pass through. If the whiskers do not touch, then the cat's entire body can pass through.

Interestingly, cats have almost no collarbone, and what they have is not connected solidly to the breastbone and the shoulder blade as it is in other animals. This makes the cat narrower and more flexible in the shoulder region. It is a surprisingly short span that must be gauged by the whiskers for a cat's passage.

CLAWS

sheathed

unsheathed

Miacids were weasel-like ancestors of modern cats.

FOR ABOUT 35 MILLION YEARS cats have been distinctively cats. Their direct-line ancestors were miacids—short-legged, long-bodied, weasel-like, forest-dwelling animals that were also the ancestors of dogs, civets, and other carnivorous animals. Cats apparently evolved along the same path as the civets, whose most familiar present-day member is probably the mongoose. Appearance of modern types of cats from these civet-like ancestors came quickly, with few transitional types known.

While cats have a family beginning that probably predates the dog family by a few million years, their intimate association with man came much later. Cats have been domesticated for only slightly longer than 5,000 years. The dog, in contrast, has been man's companion for 50,000 years or more. Even when they did submit to association with man, cats surrendered less completely than did dogs. To this day, cats have kept a strong bridge to their wild ways.

TWO TRIBES OF CATS developed in the early history of the family. The branch that prospered was composed of cats almost identical to those living today. From the start, they were intelligent, agile killers. They were well equipped to assume a leading role in a world that had become ruled by mammals.

The other branch of the family was a divergent group of animals noted most for their extremely large canine teeth. These were the saber-toothed cats, and there were a number of species.

Probably the most famous of the clan was *Smilodon,* a lion-sized but more powerfully built cat. Its sharp canine teeth were as much as eight inches long. No one knows how these big cats actually used these oversized teeth. Presumably they employed them literally as daggers to bring their prey to the ground. It is also speculated by some authorities that, despite their fierce appearance, these giant cats were much too slow-moving to be matches for the speedy mammals that were rapidly developing during their day. The great cats could overtake the slower reptiles and possibly some of the large herbivores, but they could not compete with more agile predators that developed in this same period. It is speculated by some that these giant cats may have been largely carrion feeders, using their giant-sized teeth to dig the flesh away from the bones of already dead animals. For about a million years, however, these big-toothed cats were very much on the scene, with species found in both Europe and North America.

No one really knows why, but during the Ice Ages, the big-toothed cats disappeared and became part of the geologic past. Along with many other animals of their day, a large number of *Smilodon* remains were found in the La Brea Tar Pits in California.

Wild cats are widely distributed throughout the world, but as shown above, their abundance is greatest in warm regions.

WILD CATS of 35 species and dozens of races inhabit the world's land areas. Among the large land masses, only Australasia, Antarctica, and Madagascar lack native species of cats. The domestic cat, of course, has been introduced to all places inhabited by man and has become feral in many areas, including Australia and many islands. Particularly on islands, feral cats have been damaging, annihilating native birds and other small animals in finding food for themselves.

Some species of cats live in cold climates, both at high altitudes in mountainous regions and also in near-arctic conditions in the Northern Hemisphere. Some authorities say cats evolved in cool temperate regions.

Today, however, cats are represented most abundantly both in numbers of species and in individuals in the warm subtropics and the tropics. Asia has the greatest number of species (about 20); Europe has the fewest (2). Some species have wide ranges, extending over two or more continents; others have very restricted ranges.

Wild areas are rapidly shrinking in size or are disappearing completely. Many wild creatures, as a result, are now endangered. Over half the species of wild cats face this plight. Mainly this is because of the diminished living space or destroyed habitats. In some cases, however, the cats have been hunted or trapped into near-oblivion. For some species, it is not known whether their remaining populations can respond even to special protective measures that are now being taken to preserve them.

All but a few of the very rare species of wild cats, some of which may now be extinct, are described briefly on the following pages.

Pumas range from Canada to Patagonia, inhabiting cold and mountainous regions as well as steaming jungles. They have the widest range of all cats in the Western Hemisphere, though confined to wilderness areas. As a contrast, the Black-footed Cat is found only in a restricted desert region of Africa.

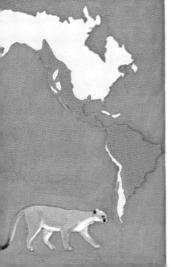

CHEETAHS, the least catlike members of the cat family, live in the savannas of Africa and southern Asia. Almost greyhound-like in appearance, a Cheetah has long, slim legs, large, muscular haunches, and a nearly doglike muzzle on its proportionately small head. In motion, the Cheetah reveals its mastery of coordination that make it, for short sprints, the fastest animal on earth. Though a Cheetah can climb, it rarely does so. Another name for the Cheetah is Hunting Leopard.

The Cheetah's reddish-yellow coat is covered with round, intensely black spots. In those that live in northern Africa, the spots tend to run together, forming almost Leopard-like stripes. A conspicuous black line extends from the corner of the eye to the mouth on each side. In Africa, the Cheetahs have a short, manelike ruff, lacking in Asiatic animals. Most authorities believe the Cheetah originated in Asia.

Cheetahs neither roar nor purr, the typical sounds made by cats. Instead, they make musical, chortling noises, almost birdlike, or they howl and bark, much like dogs. They cannot retract their claws completely into sheaths. A full-grown Cheetah male may be 7 feet long (its tail 2–2½ feet of the length) and weigh 120 to 140 pounds. The female is about a third smaller.

The Cheetah's need for large amounts of food and living space conflict with man's uses of the land, and so this cat struggles for survival in its last remaining strongholds. Many have been caught and caged for exhibition; others have been killed for their pelts. In captivity, a Cheetah becomes quite tame, even if caught after it is mature. The longevity record in zoos is 16 years, but unfortunately, many of the caged animals die of enteritis after a much shorter time in captivity. The breeding and rearing of cubs in captivity is rare.

SPEED is essential to the Cheetah in obtaining its food in the open country where it lives. Typically, it feeds on small antelopes, such as the Blackbuck, that are fleet and have greater endurance in long runs. But they cannot equal the Cheetah's speed for short distances.

The Cheetah is reported to be able to exceed 40 miles per hour within two seconds of its start and to reach a top speed of more than 70 miles per hour. It can maintain this speed for only a few hundred yards, however, and so its success depends on its being able to get close enough to its prey before making its "killing" run. Sometimes it strikes its victim's hind legs, causing it to fall, or depending on how it has approached, it may leap onto the animal's back and grab it around the neck. The Cheetah usually eats only a portion of the kills and does not return later to finish the carcass.

A cheetah's charge is astonishingly swift—
but for only a short distance.

Because they tame easily and are such skilled and exciting hunters, Cheetahs were in years gone by trained by sportsmen of India and nearby countries. The hunting procedure was much like that in falconry.

Generally mature animals, already keen in the ways of the wild, were captured to be hunters. Younger animals became too lazy and were too unfamiliar with hunting to be good sporting animals. The trained hunter was taken into the field with its head under a hood. When quarry was sighted, the hood was lifted and the Cheetah turned loose so that it could make its swift dash to bring down its victim.

Cheetahs hunt almost totally by sight and during the day or on bright moonlight nights. In the wild, two or three animals may hunt together. Young Cheetahs often climb trees. Mature animals climb only in emergencies, as when chased by dogs.

LIONS once ranged northward into Europe as well as being abundant over most of Africa and Asia. About a dozen distinct races were recognized. Now the "king of beasts" is confined to the savannas of Africa and to India, where a few hundred live in the Gir Forest.

A large male measures 8 to 9 feet long, stands 3 to 3½ feet tall at the shoulders, and may weigh 500 pounds. The female is perhaps a third shorter and weighs considerably less than the male. The male has a large mane, yellow in some and dark in others. A unique feature of both sexes is the horny "claw" in the tuft of hair at the tip of the tail. Its function is not known.

Lions are not ordinarily savage creatures. They do not command their title as "king of beasts" by force. Rather, the title comes to them perhaps mainly because of their powerful potential and regal appearance. With-

out question, the Lion is one of the most impressive of all animals. The male's roar may be heard literally for miles. It advertises his domain to other males and impresses the female of his choice. Females roar, too, but not as loudly.

Lions hunt silently and at night, often waiting at a waterhole to get their prey—antelope, zebras, and other grazers. During the day, they sleep.

Prides are the loosely organized groups of Lions. These may consist of only three or four animals, or if the hunting is good, a pride may consist of several dozen animals. One male is boss, though there may be several younger males as well as a number of lionesses in the pride. There is almost no quarreling, even over food unless it becomes scarce. Tempers do flare until the animals pair off at mating time.

HUNTING LIONS stalk their prey and then pounce to make the kill. The whole pride generally enters into the hunt. The male, if he participates, frequently goes upwind of the prey. His scent forces the prey to move off in the opposite direction—to precisely where the lionesses are waiting to make the kill.

As a rule, it is an older lioness that does the killing. She has apparently learned from past experience how to move cautiously and to be patient. The young members of the pride are often too impetuous and make their rushes too soon.

Typically the lions creep as close as possible. They do not make runs of more than 50 or 100 yards. For these short distances, they can attain a speed of about 30 miles per hour. Alert antelopes or other grazers may escape, for they are not pursued far. Lions apparently have a poor sense of smell and so do not attempt to trail their prey far. They are also a bit too lazy to exert themselves unless their hunger is great. They prefer to wait for some other unsuspecting animals to come by.

After the kill, all the members of the pride move in for a share of the feast. After they are filled, they sleep, but they may come back to the same carcass the next day to eat more—if scavengers have left any. Lions will eat a great variety of foods—from the grazers on the savannas to such strange fare as termites, fish, and even garbage. Now and then an animal discovers that it is easy to kill domestic livestock and becomes such a pest that it must be either trapped and taken to a new territory or is killed.

SLEEPING LIONS reveal an entirely different character of the giant beasts. With their stomachs full, the animals stretch out along the low limbs of trees, their legs dangling. They look as though they would tumble with the slightest stir. On the ground they sometimes sleep on their back, their feet sticking up into the air. They are perfect pictures of dead, stiff animals. The variety of positions assumed by a sleeping Lion defies description and belief, for these huge animals are masters of lazy relaxation. They spend their days resting in the shade. They hunt in the cool of the night or sometimes continue in the early morning if they have not been too successful in the dark.

In the wild, the Lion probably does not live much longer than five years. Older, feeble animals become victims themselves of predators or succumb to diseases. In captivity, however, the Lion has lived as long as 25 years. With age, the animals become more sluggish and sleep even more than usual. An old Lion depends almost totally on his younger friends to make the kills and then to allow him to join them in the feast.

TIGERS are big Asian cats, reaching a length of 8 feet or more and weighing as much as 500 pounds. They are found most abundantly in the lowlands of the tropics but range northward into the mountains of Siberia. Tigers lack manes, though older animals may get a thick, bushy neck ruff. Their basic color is a tawny yellow, with heavy brownish or black stripes that provide perfect concealment in the shadows of the forest where they live. Animals that live farther north are paler and have lighter stripes. Both black and albino individuals are recorded, and while the Tiger typically has yellow eyes, the albinos have blue eyes.

Tigers are solitary animals. They hunt mainly at night, and while they prefer deer, cattle, and similar large prey, a hungry animal will not turn away from even a mouse. They are excellent swimmers, crossing bays and

lakes to get to new hunting territory. Or on hot days, a Tiger may go into the water simply to get cool. It does its hunting at night.

Hybrids of Tigers and Lions are known both in the wild and in captive animals, but they are not common. A "tigon" or "tiglon" is a hybrid of a male Tiger and a female Lion. A "ligon" is the product of the mating of a male Lion with a female Tiger. In both hybrids, the striping is evident. and there is generally a hint of a mane in the males.

Hunted for their skins, captured for exhibits, and also killed because of their marauding, Tigers are rapidly becoming scarce. In the past two decades, a population of an estimated 30,000 has been reduced to perhaps fewer than 2,000 animals. This puts these magnificent beasts on the endangered list.

SIBERIAN TIGERS, considered by many to be the most magnificent of all the cats, are the largest and the most heavily furred of the clan. There are reports of these giants measuring more than 12 feet long and weighing as much as 650 pounds, exceeding in size the largest of the Lions. The large size of the front legs and paws is especially noticeable in Tigers. Siberian Tigers are pale. The background color may be almost cream, and the stripes are not as distinct as in other variations of the species. In the Bengal Tiger, the background color is yellowish orange, and the stripes are a very strong black.

Tigers have a reputation for occasionally becoming maneaters. These animals are the exception, the craving for human flesh apparently coming only after an older animal has become too slow to catch wild game and has made the discovery that man is easy prey and also palatable. Such a beast may kill many people before it is hunted down.

Despite its large size, a Tiger is amazingly agile compared to the Lion. It is also remarkably stealthy, passing through jungle brush with almost no noise. But the Tiger's ears pick up the slightest sounds. Tigers hunt mainly by following noises. Vision and sense of smell are not well developed.

JAGUARS are the largest cats in the Americas, some individuals measuring as much as 8 feet long (including the tail) and weighing more than 200 pounds. Most animals are about a third smaller. Jaguars are exceeded in size only by the Lion and the Tiger.

Jaguars once ranged as far north as Texas and Arizona in the United States and were found southward to Patagonia in South America. Individual animals still wander over many miles of territory, but the stronghold of the Jaguar is now the tropical lowlands of Central and South America. Their handsome coats have made them prized by hunters. Some conservationists are concerned that the population of these much-hunted animals needs careful watching to prevent extinction.

The most water-loving of the big cats, the Jaguar hunts along streams and is willing to tackle an alligator or to take a fish. It also hunts in the uplands for peccaries, deer, and other large animals. Essentially, the Jaguar is nocturnal, but like other cats, it will hunt in daylight hours if its stomach has not been filled. Despite its large size, the Jaguar is an agile climber and will pursue prey into trees. It will leap from tree to tree to capture and kill its prey. Though it typically remains in the wilderness, the Jaguar shows no great fear of man. Fortunately, accounts of animals attacking humans are extremely rare, again showing a resemblance to the Tiger.

Jaguars occur in two color phases. The most common has a yellowish-brown coat with rosettes of black spots forming a chainlike pattern. Because of the spots, another common name for this big cat is Tiger. A less common form is black, with the spots showing through only faintly. Though these big cats are kept successfully in zoos, they generally remain quite aloof and never become really docile and friendly.

LEOPARDS, though smaller than either the Lion or the Tiger, have a reputation for being much more fierce, partly because they are more lithe and athletic in their habits. The most widely distributed of the big cats—occurring throughout Africa except in the deserts and over all of Asia Minor and southern Asia—Leopards survive remarkably well in part because of their secretive habits. By day, they generally keep well hidden in the dense brush, coming out at night to hunt. If a night's hunt is unproductive, they will continue to prowl during daylight hours until their stomach is filled, sometimes roaming over 20 or 30 miles on a single hunting foray.

A Leopard's fare may be anything from a deer or an antelope to a mouse or a lizard. There are also

gruesome records of individuals that have acquired a special liking for human flesh. Leopards are swift runners and agile climbers, often waiting in a tree and then pouncing on unsuspecting prey that passes beneath. Portions of a kill not eaten are returned to later, the unfinished carcass sometimes hung high in a tree. Leopards are good swimmers, hence streams and rivers do not become barriers on their treks.

A large male measures about 7 feet long, a third or more of the length consisting of the slim, graceful tail. It weighs 100 to 125 pounds. Rare individuals may be 9 feet long and weight 200 pounds. The basic color is yellowish, with numerous black spots, but over the wide range of the species, there are many pattern variations.

BLACK PANTHERS, always with emerald eyes, are an all-black phase of the Leopard. A few occur in North Africa, but they are most abundant in Southeast Asia and in the East Indies. On some black individuals, the pattern of spots shows through faintly, as in Jaguars.

As a general rule, these are animals that live in dark, heavily forested regions. Those that inhabit more open country are lighter and spotted, with the very palest coats and almost obscure spots on animals of the open, rocky, treeless regions. Animals of the open country are also generally larger than those that live in the forests.

Similarly, the thickness of the coat varies with the habitat of the

animal. Leopards of the tropics have short fur, like the sleek, glossy fur of the Black Panther. Those that live in cold climates have much longer fur.

Leopards are such stealthy animals that their prey seldom sees them or even suspects their approach. They may wait on the limb of a tree over a well-used trail and then drop onto their victim's back as it passes below. Leopards generally eat the internal organs of the kill first and may drag the remains up into a tree for a later meal.

When young, a Leopard can be tamed, but it becomes dangerously discontented, ferocious, and untrustworthy as it matures. Leopards are not seen among the performing cats in shows.

SNOW LEOPARDS, about 5 feet long, are rare, handsome cats that live high in the Himalaya Mountains, at altitudes about 6,000 feet. Their thick coats of soft fur—gray or yellowish and liberally marked with black spots or rings—keep them warm in the alpine cold. Because of the heavy fur, their head appears small.

The habits of the Snow Leopard are not well known. They feed on goats, sheep, and smaller animals. A number of Snow Leopards have been kept successfully in captivity and have done well there. Another name for them is Ounce.

CLOUDED LEOPARDS are long-tailed, short-legged, medium-sized cats—about 3 feet long and weighing 30 to 40 pounds. They live in the jungles of Southeast Asia. The Clouded Leopard's generally gray coat, soft and thick, is spotted or striped with black. The belly is white and unmarked.

Clouded Leopards have comparatively the largest canine teeth of all the living cats. Their habits are not well known, but they apparently hunt at night, resting in trees during the day. In captivity, they try to avoid bright lights. Young cats tame easily but become untrustworthy when older.

PUMAS, also called Cougars, Mountain Lions, and Panthers, are large, tawny brown or grayish cats that purr rather than roar. They range from Canada southward to southern South America but are found only in wilderness areas. Pumas require large areas for hunting, some cats roaming over 15 to 20 miles in a night. They prefer forested regions but may also live in mountainous country—at altitudes of 8,000 to 10,000 feet in the Andes. Remarkably adaptable, they may also live in steamy tropical jungles.

The male Puma is about a third larger than the female, typical of most cats. He may weigh as much as 200 pounds and measure 9 feet long, including the tail. Pumas are relatively short-legged, and in proportion to the remainder of the body, the rounded head is rather small. Pumas may also vary considerably in size from one region to another. Those living in the tropics tend to be smaller and lighter in color than are those that inhabit cooler climates.

Though they are agile climbers, Pumas generally hunt on the ground, usually at night. They prey on deer or smaller animals, including even mice. Occasionally they kill cattle or sheep, sometimes slaughtering far more than they need. It is these few miscreant individuals that have made these big cats the objects of merciless hunts. Normally, however, they avoid human settlements.

Despite their large size and their ferocity as killers, Pumas become reasonably docile in captivity. Like other cats, they have quite individual temperaments, some being considerably more approachable than others. They are most likely to become hostile when they get older.

Though Pumas are widespread and are much hunted, surprisingly little is known about their personal habits in the wild.

SERVALS are swift African cats, 2½ to 3 feet long and weighing 30 to 35 pounds. Their coat is fawn colored, attractively marked with large black spots, and the tail is ringed with black. They have long legs, a short tail, and large ears, which give them the keen hearing needed for catching rodents and birds in the grass and brush country where they live, south of the Sahara. Servals are able to catch birds in flight by leaping five feet or more off the ground. They like to be near water or marshlands, and they are adept at climbing trees, which they often do in pursuit of prey. Those living near human settlements may make meals of poultry and young livestock.

CARACALS live in the deserts and grasslands of North Africa and western Asia. Slightly larger than Servals, weighing as much as 40 pounds, they are rated among the most graceful of all animals. Fast runners and skilled hunters, the long-legged Caracals make their meals of gazelles, birds, and other animals. Like Cheetahs, these cats are speedy but tire quickly. In India, this cat was trained as a hunting animal, also like the Cheetah, for use particularly in hunting pigeons. Caracals have large black ears with prominent tufts at the tips, similar to the Lynx. Unfortunately, these handsome cats are now becoming rare.

AFRICAN WILDCATS, also called Egyptian Cats and Kaffir Cats, occur widely throughout the northern parts of Africa. They are only slightly larger than the domestic cat, with which they cross freely. Some authorities theorize that this is one of the domestic cat's direct-line ancestors. All of the several color variations of yellow, gray, or buff have tabby markings. Also, the African Wildcat has a prominent neck ruff which it lifts imposingly to help scare off intruders. Typically, there are several rings of black around the paws and also on the lower portions of the legs. The tip of the tail is also black. These cats ordinarily do their hunting at night, spending their days sleeping and resting.

JUNGLE CATS, slightly larger and longer-legged than the domestic cat, live in southeastern Asia, mainly in India. A few occur in Egypt and other parts of northern Africa. They are grayish streaked with darker markings, white below and with a black-ringed tail. The ears are tufted, and there is a crest of hair along the back. In habits, the Jungle Cat prefers to hunt in the early morning or late evening rather than at night, roaming the grasslands and the jungle edges. Often it is found near villages, where it can prey on chickens as well as other small animals. It tames easily and mates readily with the domestic cat, of which it may be an ancestor.

LEOPARD CATS, to 3½ feet long, live in the lowland jungles and mountain forests of Southeast Asia, a few ranging as far north as Siberia. They make their homes in caves or under rock ledges. In China, they are called Money Cats because the black markings on their silvery or golden coats resemble Chinese money. They look like Ocelots and, similarly, make good pets, though they tend to remain more aloof and prefer not to be handled. Some totally reject being captives. Though their numbers are seemingly safe now, the increasing popularity of these handsome animals for pets portends a fast-coming time of crisis for the species.

FLAT-HEADED CATS are both rare and unusual. They are listed among the growing number of animals that are in danger of extinction. The general color of the body coat is reddish, but the tips of the hairs are white, as are the teardrop markings around the eyes. Little is known about the habits of these small cats. They seem to prefer hunting along waterways, where they catch mainly fish and frogs. Still more unusual, they have a fondness for fruits and berries, actually preferring them to rodents or other animal food. It is possible that this is one of their ways of getting liquids. The Flat-headed Cat is found only in Borneo and nearby regions.

MARBLED CATS have a reputation for being among the most fierce of all cats in attacking their prey. They live in the jungles of Southeast Asia. Little is really known about the life history of these small cats. Most individuals look like diminutive Clouded Leopards, though there is considerable variation in their markings. The tail is about 2 feet long, equaling the total length of the head and body. It apparently serves as a balancer when the cat is climbing.

FISHING CATS are stockily built small cats with short, stout legs and a medium-length tail. They may weigh as much as 25 pounds. The brownish-gray coat is covered with black spots and streaks, and the tail is ringed with black. Fishing Cats are not abundant, living in the brush and jungle country of southeastern Asia. Their name comes from their reported habit of catching fish by scooping them from the water with their paw. They also eat shellfish, frogs, and other aquatic or semiaquatic animals, and they are known to attack dogs, calves, sheep, and even people, particularly small children.

TEMMINCK'S CATS are medium-sized—3 to 3½ feet long—and generally have an all-yellow or golden coat, though in some individuals it may be streaked with dark and in others may be solid black or gray. These cats occur widely in Asia, mostly in the southern regions. They are partial to rocky country but are apparently much at home in trees, too.

The very similar African Golden Cat is a different species that occurs in both gold and gray color phases that commonly occupy the same area. It is now rare and considered in danger of extinction. Both cats are commonly kept in zoos.

47

PALLAS'S CAT lives in the rocky mountainous country of Tibet and Siberia. Small (1 to 1½ feet long), it has silvery, spotted, thick fur, fitting it for the cold climate. The tail is tipped with black. Most unusual, the short ears are set low on the broad head so that they are widely separated, and the eyes are high, the head lacking a rounded forehead dome. These facial features give the cat a ferocious appearance and also aid it in peering over and around rocks without exposing large amounts of its head before its eyes are in position to spot potential prey.

SAND CATS live in the deserts of Asia and northern Africa. Their fawn or yellowish-brown coats conceal them in the generally brownish landscape, and the coarse hairs on the pads of their feet help to give them traction in the loose sand. Like many desert predators, they hunt at night. They have large ears, depending on sound rather than sight to find prey.

EUROPEAN WILD CATS have survived the continent's heavy settlement by retreating to the forests where they exist in surprising numbers. Marked like the domestic tabby, they are a third larger and have a wider, more whiskery, flattened head, longer and slimmer legs, and a more sturdily built body. The blunt tail is ringed and tipped with black.

Normally active only at night, these ferocious hunters have been known to attack fearlessly both man and his dogs. During the day, these cats remain hidden in rocks, caves, or trees. European Wild Cats are reported to cross with domestic cats, but there are only a few records of the European Wild Cat having been kept successfully as a pet. In zoos, they have lived more than 15 years.

49

OCELOTS, sometimes called Painted Leopards, are handsome, docile creatures that live in the American tropics. Because they are easily caught and quickly tamed, even as adults, many have been captured and sold as pets. They have also been heavily hunted, their spotted fur used for decorative collars, cuffs, and capes. Because of the Ocelot's lack of resistance to capture and use of little craft in escaping hunters, its numbers are fast dwindling. Regrettably, as with many of the wild cats, these strikingly beautiful animals are now on the list of endangered species. They must be protected to prevent their extinction.

While Ocelots have been kept as pets over many centuries, the habits of the animals in the wild are not well known. They hunt almost wholly at night. Some animals even avoid being active on bright moonlight nights. They eat a wide variety of foods—from animals as small as lizards and rodents to as large as monkeys and deer. Those that live near human habitations occasionally make raids on chickens or small livestock. They are good swimmers and are reported to catch and eat fish.

During the day, Ocelots sleep on the ground, under rocky overhangs, in dense thickets, or sometimes tucked safely away in clumps of prickly cacti. They are agile climbers and will hunt or take refuge in trees. Sometimes they stretch out on branches to rest or to sleep.

An Ocelot's face is streaked with black, and it has numerous black rings and streaks over its body. In some animals, the centers of the black rings are brownish. The basic color of the coat is pearly buff, the underparts white. Over their wide range, there are many pattern variations. An Ocelot measures about 4 feet long, including its tail, and may weigh as much as 30 pounds. Females are a fourth smaller than the males.

MARGAYS resemble Ocelots, but most are smaller—no larger than domestic cats—and have a proportionately longer tail. They occur mainly in the tropics of Central America but range northward as far as Texas and southward into Brazil. Margays, sometimes called American Tiger Cats, are easily captured, and if taken when young, they tame quickly to become docile, affectionate pets. As they become old, however, they often lose their tempers and are then dangerous. Like the Ocelot, the Margay is in danger of extinction. It was presumably never numerous, and very little is known about the cat's habits in the wild.

PAMPAS CATS have a wide range in the grasslands of South America, particularly in Argentina and Uruguay. In much of their original territory, they are now extinct. The dark reddish streaks on the silvery coat provide concealing camouflage in the dry grass. The tail is long and gray, and the underparts are white. One race is silvery gray with no markings. Pampas Cats are about the size of the domestic cat.

Like several other small cats of South America, little is known about the habits of the Pampas Cat in the wild. It is believed to be a nocturnal hunter, feeding on birds and small mammals. Over much of its original range, the Pampas Cat is probably now extinct, pushed aside by the settlement of the land. Whether it is endangered as a species is questionable, but presumably so.

GEOFFROY'S CAT ranges from Bolivia southward to Patagonia in South America, inhabiting mainly mountainous country and avoiding human settlements. About 3 feet long, with half the length tail, it has a large head and a streaked coat.

BLACK-FOOTED CATS, not quite as large as domestic cats, once ranged widely over southern Africa but are now rare and occur only in desert regions. They are nocturnal, hence not commonly seen. The soles of the feet are black.

JAGUARUNDIS have a long, almost otter-like head. Sometimes, in fact, they are called Otter Cats, a name they live up to also in their habits. Unlike most cats, Jaguarundis take to the water readily. They are equally at home in brush and jungle country, however. Jaguarundis measure about 4 feet long, with half the length consisting of their tail. Their legs are comparatively short, adding to their otter-like appearance. The ears are small. Ranging from southernmost Texas southward through Central America to Paraguay, Jaguarundis occur in two distinct color phases: reddish brown and grayish black.

LYNXES are the most widely distributed species of the cats, inhabiting evergreen forests of the Northern Hemisphere around the world. These cats like wilderness areas, which are diminishing, and they are also hunted for their coats. For these reasons, their population must be watched closely to assure protection, though at the moment they appear reasonably safe. The Spanish Lynx, a distinct race and sometimes classified as a separate species, inhabits the mountains of Spain and Portugal. Its population there is now known to be endangered.

About 3 feet long and weighing 25 or 30 pounds, the Lynx has a heavy grayish-brown coat, necessary in the cold climate where the animal lives. Some of the long hairs in the coat are white, giving it a frosty appearance. It has a short, black-tipped tail, pointed ears with slim

tufts at their tips, and a thick, whiskery ruff of hair around its throat. The hind legs are considerably longer than the front legs so that the body slopes slightly from the rear to the front. The feet are very large and are padded, making it easy for the Lynx to walk over snow without sinking in deeply.

In North America, the Lynx feeds primarily on snowshoe hares. The population of the hares goes through cyclic fluctuations. Soon after the hares have reached a peak in numbers, the Lynx population also attains a high. Similarly, the population slumps when the hare population does, with a slight lag.

BOBCATS, which go also by the names Bay Lynx and Wildcat, are only slightly smaller than the Lynx. They live in the forests and wild country throughout North America, ranging as far south as Mexico and the tip of Florida. Surprisingly, they may thrive close to human habitations, often near large cities. Because of their secretive, nocturnal habits, they are seldom seen. Like the Whitetail Deer, these cats have prospered where forests have been cut and the land opened.

The Bobcat's basic color is brown, streaked and spotted with black, but there are a number of distinct variations over the animal's wide range. In all, the underparts are whitish. The Bobcat's feet are large but not nearly as broad as the Lynx's. A Bobcat may sink into the snow up to its belly where a Lynx pads across as though wearing snowshoes. A Bobcat's tail is short, or bobbed, which gave the animal its name; it is barred with black above and is white on the underside. The long, pointed ears are white inside the cups and lined broadly with black on the back side. They are tufted but are not as "whiskery" as the Lynx's. Fortunately for this cat, its fur is not considered valuable.

Bobcats are known for their fierceness in fights and will attack animals twice their own size. Their food consists primarily of rabbits and small rodents, but they will also prey on deer, birds, and domestic livestock, literally making a meal of whatever it appears they might overcome. Those living near settlements commonly catch rats and also feed on scraps around dumps. The diet is much more varied than the Lynx's.

If captured while young, Bobcats become quite tame. Their tempers are likely to be unpredictable when they become older, however. In zoos, they thrive well, where some individuals have lived for more than 20 years.

THE DOMESTIC CAT

The exact origin of the domestic cat is not known, but a confirmed and continuing relationship between cats and man became strongly evident about 3000 B.C. in Egypt's Nile Valley. There cats apparently first won their way to favor because they killed rats and mice that plagued the granaries and also helped rid the land of other vermin.

Eventually, the Egyptians worshipped and protected their cats, treating them as royalty. They depicted them in art and in carvings, and they celebrated cat holidays. The cats themselves were decorated with jewels. Pasht, or Bastet, an Egyptian goddess representing femininity and maternity, had the head of a cat and the body of a human female.

When their cats died, the Egyptians mourned as though a human member of the family had been lost. They mummified the cats' bodies—and also rats and mice, presumably to provide the cats with food in the hereafter. Cats entombed in this manner numbered in the hundreds of thousands. More than 300,000 mummified cat bodies were taken from only one cemetery. A study of their bodies would have helped unravel the mysteries of the cat's origin, but unfortunately, they were shipped to England where they were auctioned off by the ton to be used for fertilizer.

The origin of the domestic cat thus remains obscure, while its history since domestication is virtually unrivaled among the animals associated with man. It is theorized that the direct ancestors of the domestic cat were probably African Wild Cats, which to this day mate freely with the domestic cat. Some authorities speculate that the Asian Jungle Cat also figured in the domestic cat's ancestry, but probably no one will ever know.

Egyptians put cats into their art
forms, such as the frieze above
and the mummy below.

Pasht, the cat-headed Egyptian goddess
of femininity and maternity.

61

SPREAD OF THE DOMESTIC CAT from North Africa took it around the world within a few centuries. The Greeks were the first Europeans to keep cats. Rats and mice infested their granaries, too, and when the Egyptians refused to let any of their sacred cats be taken to Greece to combat the rodents, the Greeks began stealing them. The Egyptians made cat thievery a crime punishable by death.

The Romans in their conquests included cats among their spoils. They did not revere the cats as the Egyptians did, however, and a Roman soldier was murdered in the streets of Alexandria when he accidentally killed a cat. This episode brought on a series of reprisals that continued until Egypt was finally brought under total Roman rule. With the fall of Egypt, cats slipped from supremacy, no longer ranked as deities.

Roman legions, meanwhile, began to adopt the cat as a symbol. They respected the craft and cunning of the supple, green-eyed beasts, and though they failed to put cats to practical use as mousers, as had the Egyptians and the Greeks, the Roman soldiers managed to lose or to leave enough behind to give cats a substantial start wherever the armies went.

The precise paths taken by cats as they populated other parts of the world are mostly speculative, but along with rats and mice, they soon purred in ports wherever ships dropped anchor. They made their way overland on foot or by cart or wagon until they were common everywhere man lived. Sometimes they earned their keep by getting rid of rodent pests, but as often, the only demand made of them was to be the mysteriously beautiful creatures that they are.

In India, cats gained back some of their lost status as religious symbols. Hindus were all obliged to keep and

The main hall of Japanese cat temple, Go-To-Ku-Ji in Tokyo appears below. Its facade was covered with drawings of cats with lifted paws, all to bring good luck. Now in Japan, earthenware cats are made with a lifted paw to symbolize their ability to bring good luck (left).

to feed at least one cat, and killing a cat was forbidden. In China, where cats went by the name of *mao*, it was believed that time could be told by studying a cat's glassy gaze.

Cats came on the scene in Japan along with Buddhism. Every temple was protected from rats and mice with the minimum of a duet of cats. Those who had no cats drew pictures of them or got cat images made of wood, bronze, or similar materials. These were set where, hopefully, they would frighten the raiding rodents. The ruse did not work, of course, and oddly, this became the cause of the cat's downfall. Japanese courts legally banned the useless cats. But hordes of people who had discovered that cats are comfortable pets kept them anyhow.

CATS AND SUPERSTITIONS

Cats fell into disrepute in Europe during the Middle Ages, and many of the superstitions involving cats began during these troubled times.

Freya, a Norse goddess, was depicted as riding a chariot drawn by black cats. Christians denounced these pagan people who made cats a symbolic part of their cult. These changes removed the cat from the company of gods and put it in league with the Devil. The black cat became the particular target of cruelty to cats during these wrathful years. To this day, the black cat suggests evil and bad luck.

Old women seemed to take a special liking to cats, and it was old women, primarily, who were witches that cast dreaded spells of black magic over people and where they lived. Their cats, of course, were assumed to be their accomplices.

An incident that gave strength of evidence to this belief occurred when a woman accused of being a witch was whisked from her pyre by friends. They performed their rescue behind a screen of smoke and put a cat at the stake in substitute. Just as the smoke cleared, the scorched, howling cat escaped its bonds. The people were then convinced that the witch had changed herself into a cat and was free to avenge.

In other instances, women thought to be witches were tortured until they admitted their evil consort with cats. They were literally forced to say that they could turn themselves into cats whenever it was to their advantage.

So it became generally believed that wherever there were witches, there were surely cats, or conversely, wherever there were cats, there were witches. The two went together, and so they were persecuted together—condemned to die in bags tossed into rivers or to be burned to a crisp in iron cages swung over roaring fires. The defenseless cats suffered most. Thousands and thousands were destroyed. Entire days were devoted to cat killing and burning, as Europe slid into the frightening years of the Black Death that took its toll of millions of people. Nearly a fourth of the continent's population succumbed as rats carrying pestilence overrode Europe.

AS SYMBOLS OF GOOD LUCK, cats were restored to popularity by the same sort of magic and superstition that had brought on cruelty. These two competing elements—the people who continued to believe cats were evil spirits versus those who began to look upon them as good omens—brought the animals both kicks and caresses.

A black cat crossing a person's path, for example, was widely believed to be the sign of bad luck. Yet people who kept black cats in their houses were thought likely to be blessed with good. A visit from a strange black cat was a bad sign. Drawing the tail of a black cat over sore eyes nine times was said to cure them. Theatrical lore read bad luck into the presence of a cat on stage during rehearsals, but if a cat promenaded before the audience on opening night, the play was expected to be successful.

A black cat crossing your path is generally considered bad luck.

Black cats, like white heather, are symbols of good luck in England.

It was said that a building would stand only if a live cat were sealed into its foundation during the construction. Cats were also buried alive in fields to assure bountiful crops, and kittens were buried in gardens to keep the weeds from taking over.

White cats have in some beliefs played a role opposite to black cats. Thus a white cat crossing your path presumably brings good fortune. The person who finds the single white hair that is somewhere in the fur of an otherwise all-black cat and can remove it from the cat without being scratched has in his possession the greatest of all good luck charms.

Cats, like other animals, have also been watched as weather prophets. When a cat sits with its tail pointed toward the fire, a weather change is on the way. If it washes its face before breakfast, chances are more than slight that it will rain before sundown.

67

In **Alice in Wonderland,** Alice met the ''mad,'' grinning Cheshire Cat, which slowly disappeared except for its grin that remained for a long time after the rest of the cat was gone.

CATS IN LITERATURE AND ART

Leonardo da Vinci declared that ''the smallest of the felines is a masterpiece.'' True, their natural grace coupled with quiet, unobtrusive ways have made cats the favorites of countless artists, writers, and intellectuals. All seem to agree that the time spent with cats levels tangled thoughts and situations, for cats live an astonishingly assured and even-keeled existence.

Dr. Albert Schweitzer, the famer philosopher and medical missionary, loved cats. Writers by the score have found cats to be comfortable, inspirational companions while they work. Ernest Hemingway had a special fondness for cats and left a legacy of six-toed cats at his home in Key West, Florida. A list of writers who were or are cat lovers would include such familiar names as Edward Lear, Charles Dickens, Victor Hugo, Sir Walter Scott, William Dean Howells, Thomas Carlyle, William

Wordsworth, Mark Twain, Dr. Samuel Johnson, Edgar Allan Poe, the Brontë Sisters, H. G. Wells, Truman Capote, Paul Gallico, Tennessee Williams, and countless others. Suffice it to say, contemplative people like cats.

As a natural result, the cat has found its way into the creative outputs of many storytellers, from ancient fables with lost authorship to modern tales. They have ranged from the nonsense poetry of Edward Lear's "The Owl and the Pussy-cat" to Edgar Allan Poe's chilling horror tale, "The Black Cat," and more recently, Tennessee Williams' "The Malediction," a disturbing story of a psychotic and his strange relationship with a cat.

Ernest Hemingway ranked cats among his favorite companions, with whom to share both his meals and his innermost thoughts.

Mehitabel claimed her spirit was once incarnated in Cleopatra's body.

MEHITABEL, the creation of Don Marquis, is one of the best known cats in American literature. A stray, talkative, and usually friendly cat, Mehitabel was the constant companion of Archy, the cockroach, who wrote his tales on the author's typewriter, using no capital letters (with few exceptions) because he could not manipulate the machine's shiftlock key.

Countless stories have cast the cat in the role of the arch enemy of rats and mice, a most natural characterization. Rudyard Kipling's "The Cat That Walked By Itself" tells how the cat made a deal with man. In exchange for getting rid of rats and mice and for being gentle with children, cats were to be assured forever of a warm place to sleep and of milk to drink. This would be the limit of the cat's association with man; in all other respects, the cat would retain its independence.

Cat haters have been fewer, fortunately for the cat. Shakespeare seemed to have a great dislike for cats, for he never had a kind word for them in any of his plays and had, to the contrary, much to say against them. Julius Caesar was much afraid of cats. Cats were new animals to Rome, and Caesar never learned to understand them. Napoleon, too, could be completely disarmed by a cat's gaze, while he apparently had little fear of setting out to conquer the world.

Maurice Maeterlinck was a writer-naturalist who used words of wrath when he wrote about cats. Georges Cuvier and Georges Louis Buffon were French naturalists who spoke out bitterly against cats. Others have since joined them in denouncing cats as enemies of birds.

Puss-in-Boots, created by French author Perrault, was a clever cat that served his master by destroying an ogre and winning him both a fortune and a princess.

Richard Wittington, Lord Mayor of London, owed a large measure of his success to his pet cat.

To the Egyptians, cats were sacred. The dead were embalmed and buried in elaborate coffins of bronze or gold, like this one.

THE FIRST CATS IN ART were the Lions depicted in the famous drawings on the walls of caves in France. But the greatest richness of cat art, never since matched, came from Egypt, when the domestic cat soared to its highest peak in its association with man. The cat appeared then not only in paintings but also in countless statues, carvings, jewelry, and a variety of other useful and ornamental objects. The most delicate were tiny gold cat figurines, many of them made as amulets to be worn around the neck or hung on bracelets. Larger carvings were commonly of a mother cat with kittens. Paintings showed Egyptians putting their cats to work as hunters or as companions of fishermen in boats.

With the rise of the Roman Empire, the cat almost disappeared from art. Even in those times, though, the cat was a symbol of the most famous of the Roman legions, and it appears, too, in a number of reliefs. The cat had lost its regal position, however, and as Europe was later swept into the Dark Ages, the cat fell into such disrepute that it seldom appeared in works of art except as a figure of evil.

Cats came back in the art of Italian painters during the Renaissance. Leonardo da Vinci and many other painters added cats to their works.

Detail from Hogarth's *The Graham Children* shows a wide-eyed cat eager to get at a bird in a cage.

A Japanese painting depicts the uncontrollable curiosity of a cat that has found a spider and must decide next whether to paw at or pounce on the crawling creature.

THE CAT'S PERFECTION OF FORM   has been acknowledged by many of the world's best artists. Some have admitted that its sinewy grace somehow manages to escape capture on canvas. Good depictions of the cat by brush are really few compared to the charm and moods shown by the cat in a different art form—the photograph. Of all animals, cats have proved themselves to be superb subjects for camera study.

THE BASIC BREEDS OF CATS

Cats beget more cats—and with little difficulty. Yet no two cats are identical in looks or personality, and the challenge of those who breed cats is to perpetuate and emphasize those differences that seem desirable. The result has been a wide range of types or breeds of cats. All domestic cats, no matter what their appearance, belong to the same species—*Felis catus.*

Everywhere in the world there are special groups dedicated to the breeding of cats to produce particular types. They have governing rules on what constitutes a breed, and they keep lineage records going back to the origin of the breed. To encourage an even greater kaleidoscope of colors and coats, they hold special shows at which the cats are inspected and judged. Cat shows are held in nearly every major city, with announcements in and coverage by local papers. Even those who have no cats to enter can enjoy and learn at these events.

The classic Egyptian tabby from which all of these breeds stem is believed to have been a short-haired cat with a reddish coat striped with white. Short-haired cats are most common to this day, and they also constitute the bulk of the so-called "alley cats" that seem to roam streets without owners.

The descriptions of cats on the following pages fit the rules of no particular cat fanciers association, except as they generally accept the division of breeds into two categories: short-haired and long-haired. No one knows exactly the origin of the long-haired coat, but cats of this type apparently first appeared in Asia. The first was produced by short-haired parents, of course, but the desirable long-haired feature was then carefully preserved by selective breeding.

SHORT-HAIRED CATS

Both in appearance and poise, these short-haired diminutives of their large wild cousins of crags and jungles are unquestionably cats through and through. Though neither as exotic nor as aristocratic as the long-haired breeds (p. 94), they are by far the most abundant of the domestic cats, accounting for an estimated 95 percent of all the cats kept by man.

To qualify for shows, a short-haired cat must have ears set well apart and rounded at the tip, and without conspicuously cupped bases. The chin should be squared or perpendicular with the upper lip rather than slanted. The eyes should be rounded (Siamese excepted) and set in a broad, full-cheeked face. The nose should be broad. A good short-haired show cat has a broad chest and a muscular body. Its tail is not disproportionately long in comparison to its body, nor are its legs long and spindly. The feet are round and not large. The coat is short and thick.

A short-haired cat can have a winning personality without having perfect show features, of course. Some of the common, non-pedigreed cats are really classic in form and looks; others show their mixed ancestry. Short-haired cats are generally hardier and require less attention than do the long-haired breeds.

Some of the most common breeds and color variations of short-haired cats are described on the following pages. The listing does not cover all of the breeds, and this book treats separately the American (or Domestic) Short-hair principal color variations (black, white, tabbies, and tortoiseshells). Cat fancier associations differ in their recognition of the different breeds, and new ones are being developed regularly.

BLACK CATS are not prevalent, but they make up for it by being conspicuous. A green-eyed black cat has unsurpassed mystic majesty, but for shows, the eyes must be orange. There must be no white hairs anywhere in the sleek, shiny coat. Even the nose and the lips of the show cat must be black.

Ordinary non-show black cats usually sport white somewhere on the body. Commonly they wear a white locket around the neck. Breeding pure black cats is difficult. Generally they are not born black but begin as darkish kittens with tabby markings (p. 80). The pure black coat does not show until the cat matures, in a year to a year and a half. Because tabby markings are basic, it is not uncommon for two black parents to produce a litter of tabby kittens. On the other hand, a black kitten may appear in a litter produced by tabby parents.

WHITE CATS— pure white—are even less common than black cats. It is not rare for two white cats to produce no white kittens or for a white kitten to appear in a litter with black parents. Genetic purity is not easy to achieve or to preserve in cats (or any animals), and it takes careful breeding over a number of generations to arrive at a pure breed of white cats.

For show purposes, a white cat must not have any hair of any other color. Its nose must be pink and its eyes blue. Deafness often occurs in these blue-eyed cats. It may disappear if the kitten's eyes change color after it is several months old. With careful breeding, even this deafness can be eliminated eventually, however. White cats with yellow or green eyes are much more common.

RUSSIAN BLUE CATS may be slate blue or even almost a lavender shade. Pure breeds have the same color uniformly over their entire body. Even their lips are bluish. Their eyes are orange.

Russian blues developed in the cold regions of northern Europe where their thick, soft fur helped to keep them warm. The outer coat of hair actually stands out from the body rather than being close-pressed as in most short-haired breeds. These trim, graceful cats are noted for their mild tempers and for their willingness to be led on a leash. They are good mousers.

Russian blues are a distinctive breed that should not be mistaken for the common gray cat that is known also as a Maltese Cat.

Striped

Brown

TABBY is a name used for striped cats. The name apparently originated in the Attabiah district of Baghdad in ancient times. There the Jews made a fine black silk that was similar in markings to the striped cat's coat. In England and other parts of Europe, the silk was called "tabbi," and so the name was given also to the cats that came from the same region.

The Striped Tabby, or Tiger Cat, is gray with black stripes that are vertical on the sides from the shoulder to the base of the tail. Another stripe extends horizontally from the head to the tip of the tail. The stripes tend to break into spots near the tail, which is commonly ringed with black. Typically there are two stripes on the cheek, and the black markings form a letter "M" in the middle of the forehead. The eyes may be either green or hazel. In some cats the stripes are narrow; in others, broad.

Blue

Red

The Brown Tabby, known also as Marbled Tabby and Blotched Tabby, has a basic tan body color. The strong stripes are black, sometimes broken into swirled patterns. The eyes may be green, brown, or an intermediate yellow or hazel. The nose is reddish. Except for the swirls, the markings of the Brown Tabby are much like those of the Striped Tabby.

The Red Tabby has orange to coppery eyes. The basic color of the coat is a rich reddish orange, and the lips are brick red. Orange Tabby is another name sometimes given this variety.

In Silver Tabbies, the basic color is a silvery gray, but the tabby markings are black. For shows, the eyes should be blue-green, but there is a strong tendency for them to be yellowish. As with other tabbies for shows, there should be no white in their coats.

TORTOISESHELLS have solid patches of black, cream, and red. Males are rare, and those that do occur may be sterile. Show cats must have distinctly separated colors, without any evidence of stripes, rings, or other markings. The colors must not intermingle to make the cat brindled.

Tortoiseshells are attractive but have not been given as much attention by cat breeders as have cats with solid colors. They are not currently a popular breed.

The Calico Cat, a variation, has the same markings as the ordinary tortoiseshell, but it has white on its face, legs, and breast. In this breed, too, the males are rare. Calicos are much more common, in fact, than are the true Tortoiseshells.

KORATS are Asian cats that have become popular as pets only since about 1950. They are still not common and are expensive.

In their native Thailand, the name means "silver." It refers to the silvery blue color of their glossy coat that consists of a very fine, dense fur. Korats have much larger than average eyes, which are yellowish with a green cast. One of the most distinctive features of the breed is their almost heart-shaped head.

Korats enjoy human companionship more than do many other breeds of cats. For this reason, they make excellent pets. Like the Abyssinians, the Korats can be trained and can also master many simple tricks. Because of these desirable traits, it is highly probable that the Korat will increase in popularity.

ABYSSINIANS, according to most authorities, date directly to Egyptian times, and they do look much like the sacred cats of Egypt depicted in statues, carvings, and paintings. Their name was apparently derived from the coincidence that the first taken to Europe was procured in Abyssinia (Ethiopia).

These slender, agile cats have a grace and wildness in their manner that sets them apart from most other domestic cats. They make excellent and affectionate pets, though they may be shy and wary of strangers. They generally learn slowly but can nevertheless be taught tricks and can even be trained to perform willingly before audiences. Unlike many breeds, the Abyssinian continues to be playful after it is an adult.

A purebred Abyssinian's thick, soft coat is a brownish gray, much like a rabbit's but with the same color persisting all the way to the roots. Abys have been referred to as Bunnies or Rabbit Cats because of their coats, which are ticked with a darker color, usually black, that generally forms a stripe running from the neck to the tip of the tail. The pads of the feet are black, with the black usually extending up the backs of the legs. The fur on the inside of the legs is typically orange. In show cats, there must be no white in the coat.

The Abyssinian's head is gracefully triangular—classic in shape. The eyes may be yellow, green, or hazel; the nose is brick-red, and the tail is long. The female's voice is sometimes referred to as an uncatlike cooing, more nearly like a dove. Unlike the Siamese, however, the Aby does not make great use of its voice.

Abyssinians are not easy to breed. They produce small litters in which males generally dominate. For this reason, the Abyssinian remains among the most expensive of the breeds of cats.

REX CATS, also called Poodle Cats, are unlike either the typical short-haired or the long-haired cats. Their coat is soft, silky, and kinky. Even their whiskers are curled. They are long-bodied, agile cats with a high-arched back. The head is relatively narrow; the ears are broad at the base and not exceptionally long, the tips almost rounded.

Rex Cats are rare, hence expensive. They are becoming more popular, however, especially with people who do not like cats with straight, short hair but who also dislike the bother of constant shedding by the long-hairs. For these people, the Rex may be most satisfying, for it has a coat even shorter than the usual short-haired cat. Rexes occur in all of the colors and color combinations of the short-haired breeds. They are intelligent and very responsive to affection.

BURMESE CATS resemble the Siamese (p. 92) but are not as slim. The sleek, fine-haired coat is a rich dark brown, lighter on the chest and underparts. A champagne-color Burmese occurs occasionally in litters and has caught the fancy of some breeders.

A Burmese cat has a triangular head and rather large, pointed ears. The eyes, distinctly almond-shaped, are a rich gold or yellow. The feet are small, and the tail typically has a bend near the tip.

Burmese cats are less noisy than are Siamese, and they do not have as nervous a temperament. They are not only intelligent but also have exceptionally affectionate dispositions, which accounts largely for their recent growth in popularity.

MANX CATS have no tail. In purebreds, there is actually a hollow area where the base of the tail would fit. Manxes that are not purebred have a stump of a tail. Adding to this distinctiveness, these cats have a large, rounded rump—so prominent, in fact, that Rumpy is one of the names by which they are known. Their hind legs are longer than the front legs, and the cats hop in a rabbit-like manner rather than walking as cats normally do. They can also jump and are rapid runners. Because of their powerful haunches and strange appearance, people sometimes claim that the Manx is a cross between a cat and a rabbit. Manxes have an unusually large, round head and pointed ears. Their soft, silky coat can be any color. The origin of the Manx Cat is obscure, but it is best known as a resident of the Isle of Man.

COON CATS got their name from the striking similarity of their colors and patterns to those of a raccoon. Locally, this resemblance has led to the belief that the cat is a result of a mating with a raccoon. Though their origin is obscure, it is believed that they arrived in Maine aboard an early trading or fishing vessel, probably from a Scandinavian country. They are now mixed with native cats.

Because of their relatively long hair, these cats are sometimes described as long-hairs. The tail is particularly brushlike. In Maine, where they are most prevalent, their longer hair and furry collar help to keep them warm. Males weigh as much as 35-40 pounds, the females about a third less — both much larger than most domestic breeds. Coon Cats are considered to be excellent mousers.

HAVANA BROWNS, despite their name, did not originate in Cuba. They were first bred in England but have been recognized as a breed only since about 1960. Their name actually refers to their sleek, glossy, dark-brown color that is uniform over their entire body.

A Havana Brown's eyes are large, oval, and green, preferably dark, and the whiskers are brown, usually with a reddish or rose tinge. The large ears are round-tipped and not hairy. The tail is of medium length in proportion to the body.

In temperament, these cats are quiet and sophisticated. They may at first glance be mistaken for a Burmese because both are brown. But the Burmese is a much darker brown and also has gold eyes rather than green as in the Havana Brown.

HAIRLESS (SPHINX) CATS have such appealing personalities that their unusual looks are soon forgotten by those who own them. The result of a mutation, they are now being preserved by breeders who are interested in novelty variations.

These strange cats do not begin life completely bald. The kittens are covered with a light coat of hair that disappears soon after they are weaned. It is replaced by a dense coat of short hairs that gives the cat's body the feeling of suede. There are no whiskers. The tail is long and slim, and the eyes are gold.

Seemingly unaware that they are different, these cats are very sociable. They are much more trusting, friendly, and affectionate than are most breeds. Because of their baldness, these cats are naturally sensitive to cold weather and must be kept out of drafts.

SIAMESE CATS are generally considered to be the aristocrats of the short-haired breeds. Once the prize pets of royalty and rated as sacred, they are now the common cats in their native Thailand (formerly Siam).

A Siamese cat has a distinctive voice. It utters many cries that are not at all like the sounds made by other cats. They use their voice in "talking" to their masters and apparently thrive on being talked to in return. Siamese are among the most affectionate cats.

These cats are slim, with a rather long and distinctly tapered tail. Their sapphire eyes are almond-shaped, and in some, due to poor breeding, they are crossed. The head is almost wedge-shaped, the ears large and pointed. The fine, glossy coat is light brown or fawn over most of the body, but on the feet and most of the legs, on the tail, and on much of the face and the inside of the ears, the color is dark brown to nearly black. Kittens are nearly white when born.

Based on the colors or "points" of their dark areas, a number of variations have been developed, ranging from chocolate brown to lilac. The Red Colorpoint Shorthair, growing in popularity, is part Siamese.

LONG-HAIRED CATS

Long-haired cats are the elite of the domestic cats. Though not as abundant as the short-haired breeds, greater attention is generally given them.

Originally, all long-haired cats were referred to as Angoras. Then a distinction was made between long-haired cats called Angoras and others that were called Persians. The separation was based mainly on slight differences in coat texture. Many authorities no longer recognize this difference, making it questionable whether a distinctive Angora category really existed. All are referred to now either as Persians or simply as long-haired cats.

To qualify in shows, a long-haired cat must have a broad, almost massive body and relatively short legs. The tail must be short and heavily furred, or brushlike. The head must be round and broad, the nose short, and the cheeks full. The ears must be small and wide apart, fully furred inside and with no skin showing. All long-haired cats have long, silky coats and a definite ruff of hair around the neck. Long-haired cats shed more noticeably than do the short-haired breeds. Their owners generally groom them well and often so that the shedding is not normally complained about by their proud masters. Cats that are judged for solid colors must show no other color markings.

Most of the various color patterns of long-haired cats have coppery eyes. In long-haired tabbies, the eyes are green. White cats have blue eyes (less commonly, orange) and typically have either poor hearing or are totally deaf.

Most of the short-haired breeds of cats have long-haired complements as described on the following pages.

BLACK PERSIANS, like the black short-haired breed, are not common, nor are they as popular now as they were a few years ago. They have large, round, orange eyes. Kittens of black cats may have a brownish coat with dark roots. By the time the kittens are mature, in about a year and a half, their coats have become a rich, glossy black—if the breeder was lucky. Owners who intend to show their black cats do not allow them in the sun, which will burn the hair and turn it yellowish. They groom the cats regularly and go over them with a cloth to give the coat a sheen. For show purposes, there must be no trace of white in the coat. This is rare. Even when an all-black cat is obtained, there is no assurance that it will produce black kittens. This problem has made the breed lose favor with fanciers.

WHITE PERSIANS are startlingly attractive. Both orange eyes and blue eyes are accepted for shows. Some are odd-eyed—that is, they have one orange and one blue eye. Still others have green eyes. White cats, particularly those with blue eyes, have a tendency to be deaf—at least partly. Breeders are trying to overcome this problem and some report success.

White Persians were presumably the originals of the long-haired cats. Like all cats, they keep themselves clean and present a near-immaculate appearance even without intensive grooming. In cities, however, it is difficult for them to keep soot and grime from their white coats, and they must be bathed to keep them in shape for shows. Dry baths (p. 124) can be used to prevent them from getting colds.

BLUE PERSIANS   rate among the most popular and most handsome of all the long-haired cats. Broadfaced, these hardy, beautiful cats return your look with a disarming, almost understanding expression.

For show, as in other breeds, the bluish color must be solid, each hair uniformly bluish from its tip to its root. The collar must not be paler in color nor can there be white spots on the underside, as may occur in older cats. The colors range from light to a deep, almost lavender blue, with paler colors preferred for shows. The eyes must be coppery orange in show cats. Green and yellow eyes are common but not accepted.

The blue color is not easy to maintain in breeding. Unless both parents are pure blues, a litter produced by blue parents may contain almost any other color, commonly tabbies. Or a blue may appear in the litter of non-blue parents.

CHINCHILLAS, or Silvers, have almost silvery coats, each hair tipped with black. Their nose is red, outlined with black; the eyes are green, with blackish rims that match the black pads on their feet. As in other light-colored cats, there is a tendency for the long coat to become greasy and turn yellowish, particularly around the tail. Proud owners brush their cats with powder to absorb the grease.

Kittens, as in many other pure-color breeds, are at first marked like tabbies. Even the legs may be heavily barred with black. The stripes disappear as the kittens become older—in about two months.

In the Shaded Silver, a variety, the ticking is darker and the undercoat is pale—but not white as in the pure Chinchilla. In Masked Silvers, both the face and the paws are blackish.

HIMALAYANS, also called Long-haired Colorpoints, are the result of breeding Siamese with long-haired cats. The eyes are blue, and the coat color is like the Siamese. But the shape of the body is stocky, the head broad, and the eyes round. Lost in the breeding, too, was the wailing, demanding voice of the Siamese. The Himalayan also has a warm, affectionate personality, as do most long-haired cats. The name refers to the cat's resemblance to the Himalayan rabbit and has nothing to do with where the cat originated.

BALINESE CATS first appeared as white mutants in a litter of purebred Siamese about 1955. In personality and body shape, they are definitely Siamese, with blue eyes and a wedge-shaped head. They differ in having long, soft, silky coats. There are now seal points, blue points, and chocolate points.

SMOKES occur in two color varieties, but neither is highly popular among today's cat breeders. Smokes were much more common early in the 1900's.

In the Black Smoke, the face and the feet are black; the sides and the ear tufts are silvery. The basic color of the body is black, but the roots of the hairs are snowy white, giving the appearance that the cat actually has two coats. The white shows through as the animal moves.

Newborn kittens are all black or nearly so. The white bases on the hairs do not appear until the kittens are three or four weeks old, and the full color may not develop for five or six months.

The Blue Smoke, a light version, has a gray face and feet, not nearly as striking as the Black Smoke.

BIRMANS, the sacred cats of Burma, are extraordinarily beautiful, with lustrous silky coats. They are a natural breed that originated in Burma where for many centuries they have inhabited some of the temple grounds, protected by the priests. This breed has only recently begun to be popular in other countries.

A Birman's eyes, almost round, are a deep blue. Its ears, nose, tail, and legs are mahogany or blackish brown. Their body is beige tinged with golden orange. The original color was seal point, like the Siamese, but bluepoints, chocolate points, and other color variations have been developed by breeders. In all of the color variations, the paws remain snowy white, as though the cat is wearing gloves. The short, rather stout legs support a long, stocky body.

TORTOISESHELLS with long hair complement those with short hair (p. 82). As in the short-haired breed, males are very rare and are commonly sterile. This has made it difficult to maintain the breed.

A true Tortoiseshell has three colors— black, red, and cream. Preferably, there is a streak of red down the face. The color patches are distinctly separate. For shows, there must be no intermingling or brindling and no stripes or other tabby markings. Also, there must be no white hairs showing anywhere on the body. The eyes must be orange-yellow or coppery.

As in the short-haired breed, there is a variety in which white patches are added to the basic colors. These are considered by many to be the most attractive.

CREAMS AND RED SELFS are breeds in which the colors are quite variable. Pure stocks are rare and almost impossible to maintain. Both were in times past referred to as Orange.

Creams are yellowish-pink, and while they are not as difficult to achieve as the red color, few are bred today compared to the 1920's and 1930's when both breeds were much more popular. The Cream should have orange or coppery eyes. In both the Cream and the Red Self, the coats must be silky rather than woolly and the colors solid.

A Red Self's coat is preferably a deep red, like an Irish setter's. Both the nose and the lips are pink, and the eyes match the coat. There are many lighter shades.

LONG-HAIRED TABBIES are the counterparts of tabbies with short hair. Tabby markings are dominant, hence the breed is not as difficult to attain as are some of the others. It is not among the most popular today, however. Red, Silver, Blue, and Brown are the most common base colors. To achieve these colors in show standards may be difficult.

For shows, they are bred to bring out the richest color in their tabby markings—which must show clearly in stripes, not blotches. It is not uncommon for these or for any of the long-haired breeds to slip back to their

short-haired features. The ears may become too long, the tail too slim, or other characteristics show that make them lose the stocky, compact build that is required of the long-haired cats for show purposes. Not infrequently they will develop a white tip on the tail or a white blotch on the chest or chin. These are not acceptable features in show animals.

Tabby kittens are typically too heavily marked when first born, but these markings generally lose their strength as the kittens mature. Correct body form, which does not change with age, is more important.

CATS AS PETS

People who like cats do not have to be told why these animals make such fine companions. The cats themselves have already done this selling job. Cats are sensitive and generally undemanding, requiring much less personal attention than do most kinds of pets. They are not noisy, nor are they destructive. Cats have admirable reserve and independence. They do not serve masters out of strict obligation or blind obedience but will share pleasures. They purr to make requests—and also in gratitude.

Of all the cats kept as pets, it is doubtful that more than a fraction of a percent were carefully selected. In most cases, a neighbor or a friend offered a kitten, and some member of the family was taken by its ways. Or sometimes a homeless cat literally adopts a family. It

Cared-for pets give and take full measures of affection, whether they lack "papers" (left) or have full proof of aristocracy (above).

appears at the door, and if given food and a place to sleep, it has found what it wants—a good home. But if you did have your choice, how would you go about making a suitable selection?

The answer is strictly personal, of course. If you are selecting from a litter of kittens, do not pick the one that looks lonesome and forlorn, needing love and attention. Chances are it avoids the playful melee with others in the litter because it lacks vigor, either due to inheritance or because it is ill. Your choice should be the lively, inquisitive, sociable, bright-eyed kitten.

A kitten can adapt to a new home with ease. Its period of adjustment, if any is noticeable, will be brief. An older cat will miss its familiar surroundings and former associations. Even if a cat has strayed to your home, it will take time to get over its caution.

Show cats compete with others of their breed for various awards.

A PEDIGREED CAT?   A cat or kitten with papers signifying that its ancestry is well documented and that its breeding is true can be had only by paying for its past. Some pedigreed cats sell for thousands of dollars, but most cost much less. Knowing your cat's genealogy will be fascinating. You will probably be able to trace it back through more generations than you can your own family.

If you do decide to get a pedigreed cat, you will want to guard its papers almost as much as you do your pet. They will be important if you decide to enter the cat in shows. Or you may want to make your pedigreed cat a parent. Producing more cats of its kind could earn back its original price many times over.

MORE THAN ONE CAT? Or how about a cat and a dog? Do they mix? The answers depend partly on the personality and age of the animals and to some degree on how you handle the situation.

Older pets generally do not like intruders. They have staked out their territory—your home and its surroundings—and are ready to defend it with tooth and nail. Do not try to force a friendship. Be ready to separate the animals if they get into fights. Make certain you console your old friend, who is displaying both loyalty and jealousy. Let the animals get acquainted slowly and in their own way, which may require days or even weeks. In time they will usually learn at least to tolerate each other, establishing their own bounds and limitations on the relationship. Sometimes a dog and a cat become fast friends, but they remain belligerent if a strange dog or cat comes on the premises.

The most important relationship is the one between you and your cat. A happy cat will give many years of satisfying companionship.

Pals and playmates—but respectful of each other's rights.

FOOD AND FEEDING —a balanced diet and a regular feeding schedule are keys to your pet's happiness and health. You must select the foods. If you leave the choices to your cat, it may fill itself with foods that are most appealing to its taste. Despite common belief, a cat does not have instinctive wisdom that tells it what foods are best for it to eat.

Cats need meat, which is their source of protein. In the wild, a cat would eat mice, birds, and other small animals, and it would eat them entirely, obtaining from the internal organs and from the partially digested food in the animal's stomach the iron and additional elements that are necessary for a well-rounded diet. So while meat is an essential and basic part of the diet, you must provide the supplementary mineral and vitamin needs with other foods.

Meats of all kinds generally appeal to cats. Most meats can be fed raw, and occasionally it is wise to give the cat some liver, heart, kidney, or other organ meats. If you feed your cat horse meat, be sure to add a bit of fat now and then, for horse meat by itself is too lean. On the other hand, you must trim away some of the fat from pork. Cats also like fish, which should always be cooked and the bones removed. A meal of fish should be given at least once a week. Chicken and turkey are also favorites with cats. Give them only the meat. Be sure you remove the skin, which is extremely difficult for a cat to digest.

If you feed your cat canned or packaged foods—and the variety available is large—check the contents carefully. Good brands are well-proportioned and contain all of the necessary minerals and vitamins that your cat needs daily. Well-prepared cat foods make feeding your cat a much simpler task than in days gone by. Inferior brands

are inadequate, however, and if your cat depends on these inferior foods for a steady diet, it will not have adequate nutrition.

Milk, a traditional favorite of cats, should be offered after the solid foods have been finished. A saucer of milk each day contributes to a cat's total dietary needs. Some cats do not like milk, however, and it may make them ill. Always, a bowl of fresh water should be available. Many cats also like a variety of vegetables, both cooked and raw. These can be offered as a part of the total diet, but first make certain that your cat's protein needs have been satisfied.

A VARIETY OF FOODS is important in keeping a cat happy. A cat may eat tuna with great enthusiasm for meal after meal and then suddenly turn away from it, obviously tired of the same taste. Your cat is not necessarily being finicky. It is simply letting you know that it would like a change. Later it may go back to the tuna with just as much delight.

Give your cat some treats now and then. Offer some cooked hamburger or whatever other meat you are having for your meal. Try a piece of boiled potato or some cooked carrots, beans, or peas. Some cats also like buttered bread. They may also have quite unusual tastes—for such things as stuffed olives, cake icing, or caviar. Just don't begin catering to expensive tastes regularly. If the basic diet is maintained, no harm will come from indulging the cat in delicacies now and then.

TWICE-A-DAY FEEDING (morning and night) is generally recommended for an adult cat. Once a day is satisfactory for some cats. Cats that are catered to may try to get at least a snack every hour or two. Avoid this, at least as a regular practice.

You can let your cat eat its fill if you wish. Totally, it will consume six to eight ounces of food per day, but if you let your cat eat whenever it wishes, it may eat much more—and get fat.

Food (and water) should be at room temperature, not cold from the refrigerator. Put the food out at a specific time each day. Your cat will learn its feeding time and will be ready and waiting. Its mealtime will be an event looked forward to with an appetite. Take uneaten food away when the cat begins to wash its face, a signal that it has finished its meal. Don't let half-filled food bowls sit out to collect insects and to get spoiled.

Give each cat its own dish and take it away when the cat is finished.

Sometimes a cat will refuse to eat what you offer. If you are giving good food that makes a well-rounded diet, insist that it eat or that it gets nothing. Skip the meal, and offer the food again at the next feeding period. Your cat will get hungry enough to get over its stubbornness—unless, of course, it has lost its appetite due to an illness. You can soon determine whether your cat is sick, and if it is really ill, you should consult a veterinarian immediately.

The best measure of whether you are feeding your cat properly is the cat itself. If it eats well, remains active and happy, and has a lustrous shine to its coat, you are doing a good job of providing both what the cat wants and what it needs. Be concerned if your cat becomes listless or mopish.

LIVING QUARTERS for your cat need not be elaborate. Cats like to be warm, and they enjoy a soft bed. In fact, if you provide the kind of comfort you would like personally, you will be given your cat exactly what it likes.

Select a specific place for your cat to sleep. This should be a quiet spot away from the normal traffic in the house. You can make a bed of a box in which you have put paper covered with a blanket, or you can buy a special cat bed. Don't be surprised if your cat rejects the bed—at least for the time being. Cats are both independent and choosy. Your cat may prefer to sleep on a window ledge, on the top of a bookshelf, or in a chair. But cats also like change. They will vary their sleeping places from week to week, and eventually, if you do not force the issue, the soft, comfortable bed you have provided will probably become the favorite.

Cats appreciate having a warm, comfortable place to sleep.

When it relaxes, a cat assumes unusual, improbable positions.

In contented rest, a cat folds its front legs under its chest, closes its eyes, and naps. It can unlimber from this position in a second if disturbed. Some cats like complete quiet when they rest; others do not mind noise and may enjoy listening to music, even to the extreme of putting their head against or even inside a radio or record player to get the full effect of the sound.

A sleeping cat, completely relaxed and secure in its surroundings, may be almost as much pleasure to watch as when it is awake. When asleep, a cat sprawls. Sometimes it may roll onto its back, or it may literally hang from a bed or a chair. If the living quarters you provide are to your cat's liking, you will have no doubt about it. Your cat, whether awake or asleep, will show you how to enjoy every nook and cranny.

KEEPING YOUR CAT HAPPY should provide you with many hours of pleasure. Most pet cats live to an age of about 14 years. Some have been known to live for more than 25 years. They never get too old to enjoy play, though their interest in romping slackens with age.

Play is an important exercise and will help keep your cat in good health. Put a big paper bag on the floor and let your cat explore inside. The results are often quite comical. Or your cat may get as much pleasure from a wadded-up section of a newspaper that rattles as it is batted about. If you want to join in the play, tie a string around the center of the paper so that you can pull it this way and that. This will keep your cat's interest aroused. Slip your hand under a blanket and move it in front of your cat—and try to escape the lightning attacks. Trail a string across the floor or hang it where the cat can box with it. Or you may have a cat that likes to box with your hand (just insist that it keep its claws sheathed). Rubber balls are always fun for cats. Be certain the balls are large enough so that your cat does not swallow them.

Pet shops offer a variety of cat toys, most of them stuffed with catnip to help make them attractive. These are generally proven play items, though the objects you find around the house may be just as satisfying. Avoid painted objects; the paint may be poisonous.

One of your cat's pleasures will be bringing home gifts for you occasionally. Most often these will be the carcasses of mice or rats; sometimes they may still be living. If your cat can manage, these treasures will be brought inside to be buffeted about in a special show for you. Do not scold your cat for having put on this performance for you. Your cat is proud. It thinks it has performed a special favor for you.

117

If conditioned early, most cats will accept a collar and leash.

TRAINING YOUR CAT consists mainly of teaching it to behave in an acceptable manner. It must learn what is allowable and what is not in your house. This kind of training should be started when the cat is young so that its good behavior becomes a habit. An older cat will be more insistent on having its way, and you will discover that no animal has more stubborn determination than a cat. In a well-organized household, however, a cat soon adapts to the routine and will expect you to follow this established pattern without great variation.

Nearly all cats, if you start them early, can learn to tolerate a collar and even a leash. A few of the breeds seem even to enjoy collars and leashes. A collar bearing a tag with your name and address may help in case your cat strays. But cats do generally object to any sort of restraint. It takes gentle persistence and patience on your part to get them to respond.

Similarly, most cats (but not all) can be trained to come when you call or whistle. In the training period particularly, make certain the cat is given a reward of kind words and a tidbit for its proper behavior.

Most important for the house cat is toilet training—for using the litter box if your cat must stay indoors or signaling that it wants to go out if you live where that is possible. A kitten that can stay with its mother long enough will learn from her. Otherwise, you will have to help. When it is obvious that the kitten is looking for a place to relieve itself, pick it up and set it in the litter box or put it outside. Praise it when it performs in the proper place. Scold it when it makes a mistake— and then also show it where it should have gone. You may have to help the kitten at first in learning how to dig a hole to cover its wastes, but the learning really comes quickly. Cats become quite fastidious about their toilet habits, and they soon give no problems.

A toilet-trained cat uses its litter box.

MOST CATS CAN DO TRICKS, if you have plenty of patience and the time to teach them. Some absolutely refuse. Remember that all cats are considerably more independent than dogs. Having to perform is somehow below their dignity. But if you persist, you should be successful in getting your cat to do simple tricks.

You have to adjust your training to fit the time when your cat is in the mood to be taught, and you must also make certain not to go beyond the limits of the cat's interest at the moment. You must, in fact, use a bit of clever psychology in the early stages of the training. First you anticipate what the cat is about to do, then command him to do it and give a reward for the performance. Eventually your command will bring on the action automatically—a conditioned response.

Like the big cats in circuses, pet cats can do simple tricks.

Big cats are popular performers in circuses and other animal shows.

Kittens only four or five months old can be taught to shake hands, for example. Once they have learned such a stunt, they will continue to repeat it throughout their life if you keep them in practice. A cat that shows a willingness to learn can be taught to roll over, play dead, sit up—all of the simple tricks that a dog can do. Properly taught, it will perform on command words, expecting a tasty tidbit and a few rewarding words when it has done its stunt.

Lions in circuses and similar animal shows are perhaps the best examples of performing cats. They are really no smarter than your domestic cat, but they are given rigorous training day after day.

Even after a careful grooming, a cat puts itself in order again.

GROOMING helps to keep your cat's coat shiny and alive-looking. It stimulates the growth of hair, while at the same time removing the clutter of dead, loose hairs and preventing them from being shed on the floor or the furniture. Regular grooming is an essential for maintaining the good appearance of long-haired cats and is also helpful for the short-haired breeds, particularly at those times of the year when they are shedding.

Most cats like to be combed or brushed. Their appreciative purring gives you the good feeling that your time has been well spent. If you like to experiment and know that you have your cat's confidence, you might also try the vacuum cleaner. Some cats enjoy being vacuumed, and it is surely the quickest way to get rid of loose hairs.

Grooming should be started with kittens when they are about a month old. At least once a day go over the kitten's coat with a cloth, stroking very gently from front to back. This will condition the kitten for the brush or comb to come later.

Use a steel comb for long-haired cats. A stiff-bristled brush is good for short-haired cats. These are specially designed animal combs and brushes that you can buy in a pet store. A long-haired cat should be combed every day if possible. Be sure the coarse-toothed part of the comb goes through smoothly before you attempt to run the fine-tooth part through the hair. If the hair has become matted with oil or with burrs, first try to untangle the hair with brush stroking. If this fails, trim out the mats with scissors.

Hair is generally first combed opposite to the direction it normally lies, and then it can be worked into place smoothly. Be especially gentle when you are combing or brushing the stomach, where the hair is thinnest and the skin is most sensitive. But no matter how carefully you do the job, expect your cat to go over its coat again with its tongue to adjust itself.

HAIR BALLS are an accumulation of hair in the cat's stomach or intestine. As the cat grooms itself with its tongue, it will swallow some of the loose hair, which will be most abundant when the cat is shedding.

Normally the cat regurgitates the hair mass to get rid of it, but sometimes the matted hair, which is indigestible, passes on into the intestine. There it may cause great discomfort. The cat coughs and vomits without moving the hair ball, and the obstruction may grow large enough to cause constipation. Hair balls sometimes become so large and immovable that they must be taken out by surgery.

Grooming helps to prevent the formation of hair balls, but once the hair ball has formed, you must help your cat get relief. A milk of magnesia tablet or a teaspoon of mineral or vegetable oil sometimes helps to lubricate the mass of hair and move it through the digestive tract. Sometimes a bit of white vaseline rubbed on the cat's nose will do the trick. The cat licks off the vaseline and in this way gets the lubricant into its digestive tract.

BATHE A CAT only if it is absolutely necessary—to get rid of grease or similar substances. Cats are very susceptible to colds, and so you must guard carefully against their being wet and exposed to drafts. For washing, use a mild soap (not a detergent) and only slightly warm water. A touch of mineral oil around the eyes and in the ears will prevent soapy water from getting inside. When you have finished, rinse out the soap thoroughly. This may require three or four rinsings. Dry the cat completely, using heavy towels or even an electric dryer if your cat will permit it.

Sometimes dry bath powders will do the job best. These can be purchased at pet stores, but check with your veterinarian to find out which he recommends. Cornmeal or corn starch are also effective. Work them into the coat and then brush them out. Much of the dirt will come out with the powder.

CLIPPING A CAT'S CLAWS prevents damage to your furniture, rugs, blankets, bedspreads, and similar items. Claws too long to fit into their sheaths are also uncomfortable for the cat.

If a cat is allowed outside, it will find a tree or a post on which to scratch, dulling and wearing down its claws by its own method. Indoors, some cats can be trained to use a square of carpet or a special scratching post made of carpet, cork, or wood. Without its claws, a cat cannot climb or defend itself. Only in extreme cases should declawing be done—and then only after consulting your veterinarian. He will probably recommend removing only the front claws.

Trimming a cat's claws requires two people. One should hold the cat with one arm around the body and the other gripping the hind legs firmly. The other person

A carpet-covered post makes an excellent scratching post for a cat.

should hold both front legs, trimming the claws on first one and then the other paw. A slight pressure on the pad of the foot will cause the cat's claws to come out of their sheaths for trimming.

Fingernail clippers will do the job, but special nail trimmers are better. Get the claws in a position so that you can see through them to make certain you do not trim down to the pink, living part inside. This would be painful, cause bleeding, and possibly lead to an infection. After the front claws are trimmed, repeat the procedure to trim the hind claws.

KEEPING YOUR CAT HEALTHY is normally not a problem. With good food and a warm, dry place to sleep, your cat will ordinarily be happy and healthy. Cats, like people, do become ill occasionally, however, and they are stoic enough to refrain from showing signs of sickness until they need considerable attention.

If your cat refuses to eat (not simply indicating the desire for a change in diet), has reddish eyes and halitosis, or begins coughing and vomiting, you can be assured that your pet is really ill. Home diagnosis of the ailment is not recommended, unless you have had much experience, are absolutely confident of the symptoms, and know precisely what to do. You do not dare make a mistake, for some ailments, such as infectious enteritis, can be fatal quickly. Neither can you be absolutely certain yourself whether your cat has rabies, the flu, or simply a hair ball. The symptoms are similar.

Letting a veterinarian examine your cat is safer for you and also for your pet. Certainly it is much more comforting. Regular checkups and a program of immunization shots should be the rule, starting when a kitten is about two months old.

Simple problems can be attended to, of course, and your veterinarian can help you select items for an emergency medicine chest. A few of the common needs are listed below.

FIRST AID KIT FOR CATS

rectal thermometer	bandages	white vaseline
medicine dropper	flea spray	mineral oil, or milk of magnesia tablets
cotton balls	baby aspirin	

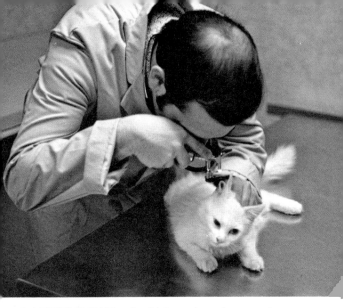

A VETERINARIAN should be selected soon after you get your pet. Kittens should have immunization shots for cat fever (infectious enteritis) when they are about two months old. Depending on where you live rabies shots might also be advisable.

In emergencies, you may need the services of a veterinarian immediately, and it is comforting to be able to turn to someone who knows your pet. Select the veterinarian carefully. Ask friends who have cats which one they have found best. It is important that he like cats. Some vets may be good with other animals but not gentle enough to handle cats. It makes no difference if he happens to be gruff with people. But watch how he handles your cat and how your cat responds to the treatment. He is your cat's doctor, not yours.

CATS HAVE ACCIDENTS AND COMMON AILMENTS

just as we do. Some of these have to do with the normal process of aging. Others may occur at any age.

FLEAS are common problems that you can attend to yourself. When you see your cat scratching regularly, chances are it has an infestation of these small, biting, blood-eaters. Do not use a household insecticide spray or dust on your cat. These are poisons that the cat will pick up as it grooms itself with its tongue. Use only dusts or sprays made for cats.

To be absolutely safe, ask your veterinarian to recommend the one least harmful. He may also suggest adding thiamine (a B vitamin) to your cat's food to help to discourage the fleas.

Getting rid of the fleas on your cat's body is only the beginning of the treatment. Fleas lay eggs in the cat's bedding, on furniture, in rugs, and even outdoors in places where the cat sleeps or rolls. Use a vacuum on the rugs and furniture. Suction all the cracks and crevices where the tiny eggs and larvae might be found. Wash the bedding. Repeat this thorough cleaning every few days to make certain all the life stages as well as the adult fleas have been destroyed.

Heavy infestations of fleas will make your cat listless and may also weaken it for infestations of worms and various skin diseases. Eliminating fleas is more than getting rid of a discomfort.

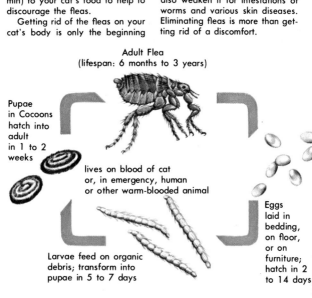

Adult Flea
(lifespan: 6 months to 3 years)

Pupae in Cocoons hatch into adult in 1 to 2 weeks

lives on blood of cat or, in emergency, human or other warm-blooded animal

Eggs laid in bedding, on floor, or on furniture; hatch in 2 to 14 days

Larvae feed on organic debris; transform into pupae in 5 to 7 days

WORMS of various kinds can infest your cat. The most common are roundworms, tapeworms, and hookworms. Their symptoms are much the same—a listless attitude, either a lack of appetite or voraciousness, a dull coat, diarrhea, and vomiting.

Worm medicine is sold in pet stores, but be careful! These are powerful cathartics, and if you get the wrong one or use it improperly, you may do more harm than good. For safety, it is wisest to have your cat checked by a veterinarian and then to follow his prescribed advice. Remember, too, that worms are spread when life stages are passed in the cat's feces, which must be destroyed to protect other pets and to prevent reinfestation of your patient. Change the bedding daily.

SKIN PROBLEMS include ringworm, which is caused by a fungus. Hair is lost in circular patches over the cat's body, and the skin in the bare areas becomes scaly. These spreading, itchy sores are irritating and cause a cat much discomfort. They can also be the entry sites for various bacterial infections.

Tiny, spider-like mites may also infest cats, some kinds occurring only in the ears and others only on the head or on the body. Cats can also get lice, or if they are free to roam outdoors they will surely pick up ticks from time to time. Unless you had experience with these various parasites before and are confident that your treatment is correct, check with your veterinarian at least the first time you treat an infestation.

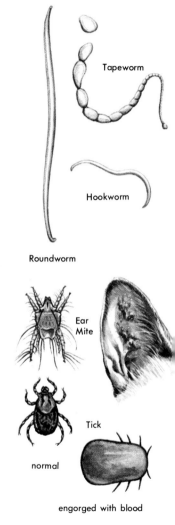

Tapeworm

Hookworm

Roundworm

Ear Mite

Tick

normal

engorged with blood

INTERNAL DISEASES OF CATS are generally serious and must be treated by a veterinarian. If your cat does not have its usual vigor, it may be best to get professional advice. Internal disorders are usually manifested by vomiting, diarrhea, or similar very obvious symptoms, however. Take your pet's illness as seriously as you might your own, for when a cat appears to be sick, it is probably much in need of attention.

RABIES is not common in cats, but it does occur. There is no cure for rabies after it is contracted. Immunization shots are advised if the cat will be wandering where it might contact animals that could transmit the disease.

FLU, a common ailment in cats, has symptoms much like those of a cold in humans, including a runny nose and sneezing. If your cat appears to have a cold, keep it inside and away from drafts. If the condition persists or appears to worsen, see your veterinarian. Do not neglect your cat, believing that its "bad cold" will go away on its own. Your pet may have developed pneumonitis, a deeper infection that requires treatment with antibiotics. This highly infectious disease is transmitted from cat to cat, hence it may be wise to have an annual immunization shot to prevent recurrence.

PANLEUKOPÉNIA, or feline infectious enteritis, is an extremely dangerous disease, almost always fatal to kittens and also to many older cats. Because the symptoms may be like those for flu, it might be overlooked. Treatment must be given as soon as possible to save the cat. This involves a program of antibiotics and blood transfusions. Kittens should be immunized when they are seven to nine weeks old. This is usually accomplished with two shots, sometimes with one.

URINARY AILMENTS—cystitis, an inflammation of the bladder, and nephritis, an inflammation of the kidney—commonly affect cats, particularly males. These ailments can usually be detected when the cat has difficulty relieving itself. It may be "humped" as it walks. Because of the danger of uremic poisoning, take the patient to a veterinarian immediately.

INFECTIOUS ANEMIA is probably passed to cats by fleas. It is caused by a parasite that destroys red blood cells. In time the diseased cat loses its appetite, becomes thin and listless, and develops a fever. Cats with this disease generally have some poor and some good days as the infection builds up. For this reason, the disease has often progressed to a serious stage before it is detected. Treatment with antibiotics and with vitamins is effective in the early stages and to a lesser degree in later stages. Controlling fleas, probably is most important.

TOXOPLASMOSIS is a rather common parasitic disease that appears in cats and other warm-blooded animals. The eggs of the parasites, protected in cysts, are passed out of the body in the feces. Cats are particularly good transmitters of the disease because they carefully bury their feces, giving the eggs the necessary two or more days for incubation. The eggs then remain viable and in an infective stage for as long as a year.

The egg cysts may also get into a host's body (cat, human, or other animal) if raw or rare meat is eaten. Pork and mutton tend to

be higher in the number of cysts than beef.

In human beings, the greatest danger is the contraction of the disease by pregnant women, for it may result in birth defects. In other cases, an infection generally has only mild consequences. For protection, a pregnant woman should not accept a new cat in the house, because its previous diet will not be known. If there are cats in the household already, the pregnant woman should have someone else empty the litter box daily. This will dispose of the feces (perferably burned) before the eggs are infective.

The cats in the house should not be given raw meat, and the woman should leave all of the gardening chores to other members of the family until her baby is born. If she visits another house where there are cats, she should avoid petting them.

YOUR QUEEN CAT CAN HAVE KITTENS soon after she is eight months old—if you permit it.

Many pet owners prefer to have their cat spayed or neutered as soon as it matures, which is during the fourth or fifth month for a female and the eighth month for a male. This operation is simpler for the male than for the female, but it is not difficult or dangerous for either. It is not expensive. Special clinics for neutering cats have been established in some metropolitan areas.

Spayed or neutered cats do not roam at night. They do not join the crowd on fences or roofs in howling, yowling choruses. Males do not get into fights that sometimes result in bad cuts that become infected, nor are they frustrated by being kept indoors where their spraying may become virtually intolerable. Females also suffer both mental and physical difficulties if their sexual activities are inhibited. But when the urge is eliminated by spaying or neutering, both sexes become docile stay-at-homes—and sometimes get fat if their diets are not watched carefully.

Allowing your cat to have kittens may be part of your plan, particularly if she is pedigreed. By selecting your cat's mate, you can control, at least to some degree, the kind of kittens she will produce. Otherwise she will surely try and probably find a mate herself when she is ready, which is usually about twice a year. Her kittens may be surprising colors and patterns.

Kittens are born in about nine weeks. During her pregnancy, the mother-to-be goes about her normal life, but she tends to become a bit more cautious and may sleep more during the last days. During her pregnancy, she will eat more food and should also be given extra milk to help replace the energy drain and calcium losses from her body.

A mother cat takes good care of her kittens, preferring no help.

About a week before the kittens are to arrive, the expectant mother begins looking for a place to have them. You should help her, for if you do not, she may select a closet, a shower stall, or even your bed.

A large cardboard box will do. It should be long enough so that she can stretch out. You can cut away one side, but leave the edge high enough so that the kittens will not be able to crawl out. It may also be best to leave the top on so that the nest is rather dark inside. You should be able to open it easily to get at the kittens, however. Be sure to put the box in some out-of-the-way place so that the mother and her kittens will not be disturbed. Put several layers of torn or shredded paper in the bottom and then let the expectant mother scratch around to arrange the nest to suit her. Put a blanket or cloth over the paper and also an old towel to be used when the kittens are born.

This kitten, with its eyes still shut, is only about a day old.

MOST BIRTHS go to completion without difficulty. The number of cats born naturally are good testimony of this fact. But in this case you have a vital interest in one particular cat—because she is your pet. If she is pedigreed, you may also have a special interest in her kittens. If she appears to be having trouble (one kitten should be born every half hour), you may want to call a veterinarian for his advice or help. Occasionally the births are not easy, and he can give her professional aid, including a Caesarean if it is necessary.

WHILE GIVING BIRTH, your cat will probably want your company. She will need the comfort of reassuring words, but do not help her unless it is absolutely necessary. The process usually is completed in about two hours, but occasionally it will take eight to ten hours.

Each kitten emerges head first, still surrounded in a plastic-like sac. The mother will instinctively remove this sac. If she does not, then you should do so immediately, for the kitten cannot breathe until it is free of this encasement.

Similarly, the mother will probably cut the umbilical cord herself, but if she does not, then you must do it. The cord can be pinched off or, better, trimmed with a pair of scissors (sterilized). It should be severed about an inch and a half from the kitten's body. Squeeze the end together for a few minutes so that there is little loss of blood.

The mother cat will immediately wash each of her newborn kittens. She appears to do this roughly, but she is instinctively stimulating the kitten's breathing process and is helping to stir the flow of blood. You must be watchful at this stage, too, for if a kitten shows no sign of beginning to breathe, you should lift it out and hold it upside down for a few minutes. Mucus that may have collected in its breathing passages will then move out of the way. At the same time, rub the kitten gently but briskly with a towel to start its circulation.

Each newborn kitten can be put in a smaller box that you have earlier placed at one end of the nest. The box also contains a hot water bottle with warm (not hot) water to keep the newborn kittens safe and warm while their mother continues to give birth to others. Four is a common number in a litter, but there may be as many as eight. Rarely are there more. If a kitten begins to cry, indicating hunger, you may put it to one of the mother's teats from which you earlier trimmed away the hair.

The mother cat will eat the placenta, or afterbirth, that comes after each kitten is born. This is normal and should not alarm you. You should make certain, in fact, that an afterbirth does follow each birth. If it does not, you should draw it out with your finger if possible. It may cause infection if left inside the mother.

Keep a bowl of water available for the mother cat. If the birth process continues over many hours, you may also want to provide her with some milk.

A mother cat meticulously cleans her kitten with her tongue, starting at their birth and continuing for many weeks afterward.

KITTEN CARE should be left to the mother cat at first. She can attend to keeping them well fed and washed much better than you can. She will not be too pleased, in fact, if you interfere, though a pet that feels secure will be tolerant. Alley cats that give birth to kittens outdoors may move their family several times to hide them away from prying people.

Kittens are at first deaf. Within a few days, they can hear and also smell and taste, but their eyes remain shut for a week to ten days. It is best not to take them from the mother until they are weaned—at six weeks to two months. By this time they will have their first set of teeth.

THE EYELIDS of a baby kitten tend to stick together due to normal secretions. This may be especially true with an orphaned kitten who will not have its mother to help keep it clean. You can wash the eyes with moist balls of cotton or with a soft cloth. Be very gentle. The sticky secretions should be absorbed without rubbing the eyes. If this does not work, ask your veterinarian to prescribe a special solution for cleansing the eyes.

TWENTY-SIX BABY TEETH should be in place within approximately a month. These remain until the kitten is about six months old, when permanent teeth push them out. At the same time, four additional teeth appear. Some kittens get their teeth earlier than six months, some later. While teething, the kitten may not eat well and will be easily irritated. Occasionally a veterinarian is needed to help get the baby teeth out of the way.

IF KITTENS ARE ORPHANED, you must take over the duties of the mother. At first, they should be fed only milk. Diluted cow's milk is satisfactory, but your veterinarian (select one early who can give advice and help with any such problems) can give the ingredients and proportions necessary for a formula if you prefer.

Milk can be fed from an eyedropper or from a doll's bottle, if the kitten will nurse. Sometimes you can help a kitten get started by letting it lap milk from a soaked cloth or from your finger. Or you can rub some milk over its lips to give it a starting taste. Do not force a kitten to take milk too rapidly, and do not allow it to drink too much at one time. Rather, feed it about six times a day— that is, every four hours.

A mother cat licks her kittens after each meal to clean them. This gentle massaging with her tongue also helps the digestive process and brings about an elimination. If the kitten has no mother, you should follow each of its meals with a gentle rubdown with a warm, moist cloth or a sponge. Massage toward the rear. The kitten will probably eliminate. Be prepared for this event. Do not have the kitten in its clean bed or on your lap.

A baby kitten will drink milk from a doll's bottle.

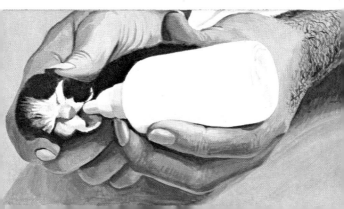

Kittens eagerly lap up their share of milk from a bowl.

AT FOUR TO FIVE WEEKS, kittens can take small amounts of solid food. Baby cereal, bread soaked in milk, or special starter kitten foods that can be bought in pet stores should be used. The kittens should be fed four or five times a day. If they are still nursing, three meals a day will do.

Even when they are weaned, at about eight weeks, refrain from giving kittens many solid foods. They have small stomachs but gluttonous appetites. Very soon you will learn that kittens, like adult cats, have definite food preferences. Make certain their meals are well-balanced, however. They will need meat and milk (some kittens later refuse milk), and they may like vegetables. Most prepared cat foods contain basic needs. Always make certain that your kittens have a bowl of fresh water, which is changed at least once a day.

A WARM PLACE TO SLEEP must be provided. If your kittens are with their mother, this problem is solved automatically, of course. They can not only snuggle close to her warm body but also have snack food within easy reach. But if the kittens are orphaned or if you have taken them from their mother, the task of making them comfortable becomes yours.

A box or a blanket with a towel or a piece of blanket inside will do. Cut at least one side low enough so that the kittens have no difficulty climbing inside. Put the bed in a place where it will not be in a draft, lifting it a few inches off the floor if necessary. Finally, make certain the kittens learn that this is where they should sleep. If the place you have provided is warm and if the kittens' stomachs are full, this lesson will require no effort.

With their stomach full, kittens snuggle and sleep.

BEGIN TRAINING KITTENS EARLY. Don't let them develop bad habits. If your kitten persists in climbing on a table or in sleeping on the stairs where it can be stepped on or possibly trip someone, insist that it does not do these or other objectionable things. Be firm—but do not whip your kitten. Like older cats, a kitten does not respond to harsh treatment. Say NO loudly. At the same time make a loud noise by swatting the stairs or the table with a folded newspaper. A kitten does not like loud noises and will soon learn to avoid what causes them to be made.

Toilet training should be started as soon as the kitten is big enough to be about on its own, usually when it is about a month old. If the kitten is still with its mother she will take care of it until then. If the kitten is orphaned or if you took it from its mother early, then you will have had the chore of cleaning the kitten regularly, as the mother would. Use a soft cloth.

When it is still very young, however, a kitten can be trained to go outdoors, or if this is not possible, it will learn to use a special pan or box (p. 119). This really comes naturally for the kitten. All you need to do is provide the place. Make certain that you use a box or a pan that can be cleaned easily every day. Keep the box in the same place so that the kitten knows exactly where to find it. If the kitten makes a mistake, as it will at first, scold it. As you do, show the kitten again the place you have provided. A kitten really learns quickly and willingly. Like an adult cat, it is embarrassed and obviously distressed when it does something that displeases you.

A kitten does not shed hair as much as it will when it is full grown. Nevertheless, start brushing and combing it early in its life so that it becomes accustomed to the process. Getting rid of loose hairs will keep them out of your way and also out of your pet's stomach where they may collect and form a hair ball.

A well-fed kitten kept in clean, comfortable quarters will be bright-eyed and healthy—on its way to becoming the perfect pet, quiet and contented.

A cat that was conditioned to gentle brushing as a kitten purrs appreciatively during its daily grooming in later life.

KITTENS ARE PLAYFUL, a part of their growing-up education that, in the wild, prepares them for getting their food and protecting themselves. The exercise strengthens their muscles and also gives them skill in fighting tactics. But kittens make their education fun for themselves and for anyone who is watching them.

If a kitten has brothers and sisters or is still with its mother, its play will be taken care of regularly. You will see even in a still cottony kitten the crouched, stealthy stalk that is typical of cats. This is followed by a swift, rushing attack. If there are two kittens, a wrestling match ensues. On its back, a kitten makes powerful digging kicks with its hind legs. Imagine what such kicks would be like from one of the big wild cats equipped with giant-sized, hooked claws!

If your kitten is alone, you will have to be its playmate from time to time. Children generally get as much pleasure from these sessions as does the kitten. Usually, in fact, children must be cautioned not to play too rough and to hold down the play periods to half an hour or less. These can be repeated several times a day, though.

A kitten must learn not to play rough, too. At the very beginning, a tiny kitten will unsheath its ten needle-sharp claws as it plays. If the attacks are being made on your hand, the play soon becomes painful. Scold a kitten when it claws you. It will soon learn to keep its claws in.

Cats that live in the country or in suburban areas can go outdoors daily for walks or to bask in the sun. Those that live in apartments may be confined to the building, and they can suffer from the lack of exercise. Daily walks do help keep a cat in good health. This can be done only if the cat is willing to wear a collar and will submit to a leash. If this is the only way your cat will be getting exercise, you can start preparing it for the collar and leash while it is a kitten.

Pet stores offer a wide variety of toys that will delight your kitten. Many include a stuffing of catnip. You can find numerous objects around the house to please your kitten, too. Like older cats, a kitten will like a cardboard box in which it can hide, scratch, and then lounge. Paper sacks, crumpled pieces of paper tied to strings, feathers—these will keep a kitten happy hour after hour by itself.

If you do not give your kitten toys, it will find its own—and this may be dangerous. The curiosity of an adult cat is exceeded only by that of a kitten. Make certain it does not chew on an electrical cord, amuse itself by knocking items off a vanity, get itself locked in a cupboard, or get stepped on as it follows you around the house. Kittens often get into predicaments that demand your help, but each experience makes them a bit wiser about their world.

KITTEN TO CAT, A HUNTER. This is the natural sequence in nature. It was as hunters that cats first earned their keep with Egyptians. The cats not only protected the granaries from rats and mice but also discouraged birds from eating fruit. As mousers, cats are still appreciated, but their reputation for killing birds has put them in the disfavor of many.

Each cat is different, however. Some are good at catching mice and rats; others do not want to be bothered. Some derive great pleasure from hunting birds, while others can sit by a bird feeder and scarcely give the birds that come there a second glance. Still others will practice their inherited art of hunting from time to time and then lose interest, just as some people pursue a particular hobby with great enthusiasm for a while and then suddenly shift to another. It is a mistake to indict all cats for the miscreant behavior of a few.

When a cat does go hunting, it combines its cunning with the remarkable anatomical features that make cats master hunters. These include its keen senses of hearing and sight, its ability to move silently on well-padded feet, and its swift, short-distance runs that enable it to overtake its prey almost before they have had time to muster a startled escape. In hunting, cats are "loners." Their hunting methods are not developed for group work in packs as dogs often do, though some of the wild cats do cooperate in making their kills. The cat's typical method requires great patience. Determined to make its catch, a cat may sit silently for an hour or even longer, not budging from one spot until a mouse or a rat loses its caution and comes within range of the cat's well-measured pounce.

A pet cat rarely hunts to get meals. Many are so well fed, in fact, that they have great difficulty being inspired by the thought of a hunt, strictly for sport and the sense of accomplishment.

"Wild" or feral domestic cats have been killed in large numbers in several states and the contents of their stomachs analyzed. Birds made up a very small percentage of their meals. This is small consolation to the bird in your backyard if your cat suddenly gets the notion to make that bird its quest. Nor does it placate neighbors who think your cat is driving all the birds away from the area.

To take care of such situations, you can get a collar with a bell on it. This will announce every move your cat makes, and after the cat learns that it can no longer sneak up on its prey, it will turn its attentions elsewhere. It will probably learn to use the bell to announce that it wants in or out of the house. Some cats seem to appreciate having this signaling device.

AS A CAT BECOMES OLDER, it may begin to require special attention. When is a cat old? This varies with the individual. It depends on the cat's heredity and also on the kind of life it has led. At ten years, however, a cat is becoming a senior citizen. Most house cats live to be twelve or fourteen years old; some pets live for more than twenty years. The symptoms of aging in cats come on gradually.

Older cats are not as spry as they once were. If younger cats are around them, the spirit of play may return from time to time, but the older cat spends increasing amounts of time resting and sleeping. Make certain that your old friend has a warm, comfortable bed in which to curl up and dream of other days. If your pet gets caught in the rain, dry him with a brisk rubbing before he settles down for a snooze.

If you permit it, cats will eat more than they should, and in older, less active cats, this can result in fatness. Obesity is no better for cats than for humans. Watch your cat's weight. If he begins adding ounces and then pounds, reduce the amount of food he gets. Keep the diet well rounded, of course, and pay no attention to the complaints that will come first. After a few days, your cat will adjust to the restriction on food intake.

When your cat begins drinking more water than usual, be on guard for a kidney ailment. Degeneration of the kidneys is not unusual in older cats, and if it occurs gradually, it causes no great difficulty. But it is wise to have your veterinarian check your cat's condition and to prescribe a treatment if it is necessary. Kidney diseases can be serious and it is not uncommon for tumors to develop in the kidneys of older cats.

Finally, just as in humans, loss of teeth and at least partial deafness are likely in older cats. You may have to begin serving softer foods—even kinds that can be "gummed"—and you will probably have to shout louder when you call your friend at the door. But if you have had your pet so many years that these infirmities have set in, you will not mind these slight inconveniences to make him happy in his last days.

A grayed, "senior citizen" cat spends many hours sleeping.

SHIPPING A CAT OR A KITTEN may be necessary. This will occur if you are not taking the trip yourself but are sending the cat or kitten to someone. Or you may also be going on the trip but are not permitted to have an animal in the passenger area.

Shipping by bus or by train is advisable only for short distances. For longer trips, the airplane gives the fastest, smoothest ride. But in all instances, the responsibility of making sure your cat or kitten has a safe and satisfactory trip is really yours.

First of all, do not make the shipment unless the connection is direct. Don't risk having your cat or kitten spend unnecessary hours of waiting in layovers and perhaps even be missed. Make all of the shipping arrangements several days in advance so that the boarding procedure itself is very brief. Stay with your cat or kitten as long as you can to keep it comfortable and to make certain it is being loaded properly.

If you can do so, make the shipment collect. When payment is yet to come, the handling of the cargo tends to be swifter and gentler. Also buy adequate insurance. The cost is not great, and it will give you much peace of mind to know that your cat or kitten is being given careful handling en route.

You can either rent or buy a carrier. If shipping is likely to come up often, it may be best to purchase a carrier of your own. In this way, you can keep the carrier in good condition and can also have time to get it ready for each trip. You can even condition your passenger to spending time inside it so that the space is not unfamiliar when it comes time for the actual trip. Before the departure, put some paper on the floor of the container and perhaps even shred some of it. This makes an easily disposable litter that your animal may find useful

Special carriers for cats get them safely to their destination.

during the trip and is easy to clean out. For short trips—and most of those by airplane do not require many hours—it will not be necessary to provide food. If you wish, you can put some dry food in the carrier. Some people like to put the rations in small plastic bags that are stapled to the sides of the carrier. If your cat or kitten becomes really hungry, it will find these packages, and getting inside the bags gives it something to do to occupy its time during the trip.

Most important, make certain that someone will be on hand to meet your cat or kitten when it arrives at its destination. If this cannot be arranged, it is best to wait and make the shipment at some other time. A wait at a terminal can be indelibly frustrating for a pet.

Some cats enjoy riding in automobiles on short or long trips.

TRAVELING WITH CATS is sometimes less expensive and is certainly more comforting than leaving them with friends or boarding them. If you think travel is likely in your cat's life, start the conditioning early, for an older cat may never adjust to riding in an automobile.

Kittens can generally be trained at least to tolerate automobile trips. First let them play in the car while you just sit there. After several such experiences, start the motor on the next visit to the car. This gets them accustomed to the sound of the engine. If all goes well, begin taking short trips—around the block or through the neighborhood.

Some cats learn to enjoy car traveling thoroughly, especially if they know that food and a litter box go with them. Pet stores can even provide you with a cat car seat so that your pet can sit up high and see out the windows just as you do. But remember to keep the windows closed far enough so the your pet cannot leap out. The urge to have a look around outside may come when the car is moving or when you have stopped for a traffic light or a stop sign.

Some cats never become comfortable in a moving car and will worry the driver and passengers by pacing around inside. For everyone's comfort, these pets should be transported in a cage or carrier. It should be large enough so that the cat can move around and should have screens at the top and sides. But preferably, it should not be so large that it cannot be carried by a handle on top like a suitcase. This will make it easy for you to take the cage from the car to the motel room or wherever you put up for the night.

Even for cats that do not have to be caged, a carrier is still advisable for transporting them when you are out of the car. Collapsible carriers, much like duffle bags, are convenient for use in these circumstances. It is important to keep your pet confined or on a collar and leash when you are in a strange area. It is easy for a frightened, bewildered animal to panic and run off. You may have difficulty getting your pet to respond to your calls or may not be able to find it.

Use a carrier to keep your pet from getting lost in a strange place.

BOARDING YOUR CAT may be necessary when you go on trips, particularly if your cat is a poor traveler. If you do not plan to be gone long, perhaps you can get a friend to come to your house to care for your pet. It will be happier with food, water, and a litter box at home. Or maybe a friend will offer to take your cat to his home during your absence. If you have accustomed your cat to ''visiting'' now and then, this may be possible, but there is also a danger that your pet will run away and go back to his home.

Cats are not especially good boarders and would much prefer to stay in familiar surroundings. If your trip will be long, however, it is probably best to find boarding facilities.

If you do not know a good place, call your veterinarian to get his advice. Some veterinarians have accommodations for instances of this sort, and you may be able to combine your absence with a medical checkup for your pet. You might also find out where friends who have had the same problem have kept their cats.

Most important, find a clean place so that your pet is still healthy when you return. Accept the fact that your cat will not be happy until it is home again.

ABANDONMENT of cats is cruel and malicious—and a much too common occurrence. Cats are extremely sensitive. They thrive on kindness and pampering. Most of those forced to feed for themselves may manage to survive, but they are usually unhappy, frightened, skinny, often diseased and neurotic creatures. Through no fault of their own, these are the cats that give their kind a bad reputation generally. They become the shadowy, slinking animals seen in alleys and around garbage cans and dumps. They howl and fight, steal food at market places, kill birds in yards and parks—living up to the social outcast image thrust upon them.

Cats are abandoned for a variety of reasons, none of which are good ones. A cat taken to a summer cottage may be left there because the family is simply tired of the pet. A bag of kittens is dumped in the country, perhaps with the hope that someone will feel sorry for the waifs and take them in. But this rarely happens. When a family moves, they may have no place for their cat in the new home. They leave it behind.

Never abandon a cat or kittens. If they are unwanted, contact an organization that can find a home for such animals or that can give them humane treatment.

FERAL CATS are domestic or house cats that are "wild." Unlike the recently abandoned cat, or stray, that is generally anxious to find a home again, a feral cat is fiercely independent. It shuns people, though it may steal its food at the trash can or the garbage dump. "Wild" cats of this sort are common in most large cities and in many rural areas.

Feral cats get their start when two strays produce a litter of kittens that grow up never associating directly with humans. These kittens find mates among their kind,

153

Cats are remarkably capable of taking care of themselves in the wild.

and soon several generations separate the cats from human contact. Each adult female is capable of producing two or three litters per year. Authorities estimate that the total number of feral cats in the world is well into the millions.

These "wild" cats become carriers of disease that can spread to pets. They are also the notorious killers of birds and small game animals as well as some poultry and livestock. Their menace becomes most obvious on islands, where birds and other wildlife may be destroyed. Ground nesters, such as seabirds, suffer especially. Feral cats threaten to become a plague in Australasia where no cats were native. But wherever they exist, feral cats are a result somewhere in the past of the abandonment of a cat or cats that would have been happier on the hearth.

CAT CANS AND CANNOTS

Cats move in such a shroud of mystery, always keeping a psychological distance between themselves and their human companions, that many myths have evolved around their behavior and powers. At the same time, cats are indeed animals endowed with unusual capabilities. Separating fact from fallacy is therefore often not simple. Listed here are a few of the common beliefs about cats, some of them true and others false.

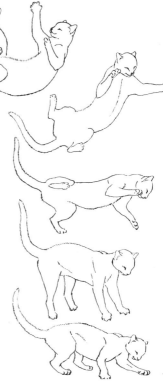

CATS CAN USUALLY LAND ON THEIR FEET if they happen to fall from a tree, roof, or other elevation with their back down. They do not always manage to get turned over in time, but by flipping their tail and twisting their body, they make an astonishingly quick flip in midair. A cat can be badly hurt in a fall, naturally, but its tough muscles give it surprising bounce that is a protective feature no matter whether the cat lands on its feet or happens to miss. But a cat definitely has an uncommon sense of balance. If the fall is far enough to give it time to turn, it will almost always land on its feet.

Cats do not have nine lives, a belief that has come about only because cats do manage so often to survive troubles that would kill other animals.

CATS CANNOT SUCK A BABY'S BREATH and kill it. This is one of the very common beliefs that is absolutely untrue. Because cats like children and many cats also like to lie close to a human being, it would not be unusual for a cat to lie next to a baby. Between the moving around of the two of them, they might indeed get into a position in which it looks as though the cat is trying to suck the baby's breath. Or the cat may actually lie on top of the baby so that the baby could cough and cry, alarming a mother.

It is best to keep the cat away from the baby, mainly for sanitary reasons. When the baby becomes a mischievous child, be equally concerned for the cat's safety at times. Cats and children ordinarily become great companions, with the cat taking much more abuse from the child than it would tolerate from an adult.

CATS CANNOT SEE IN THE DARK. No animal can actually see in total darkness, for seeing requires the existence of at least some light. But a cat can see in extremely dim light. It can open the pupils of its eyes very wide to let in whatever light is available. A special coating, the tapetum lucidum, at the back of the retina reflects this minimum of light so that it is fully utilized.

CATS CAN FIND THEIR WAY HOME

from long distances. They have a remarkable, little studied homing instinct that enables them to travel hundreds of miles through strange territory to return to familiar surroundings.

This does not mean that when a family moves and takes their cat with them there is great danger that the cat will run away to go back to its old home. Despite their seeming indifference, cats do have great affection for their "family," and it is rare for a cat to stray intentionally from the people it associates with its home. Contrary to an age-old belief, cats really like people more than they do places.

CATS CAN SHOW GREAT CONCERN

for people. There are recorded cases where cats have saved people's lives by waking them when a house was on fire or there was a gas leak. They have also alerted them to the presence of scorpions, poisonous snakes, and other dangerous intruders. Their affection and understanding of their own family is demonstrated in many ways. They know the usual voices and sounds in a house, but if a strange voice joins the conversation, the sleepy cat suddenly becomes wide awake. A cat does not move at the sound of the family car in the driveway, but a strange car puts it on alert immediately. A cat is almost always hostile to new pets in the household, but if the pet is an obviously accepted addition, the cat learns to tolerate it and may even become friends.

MORE INFORMATION

Ames, Felicia, **The Cat You Care For,** Signet, The New American Library, New York, 1968

Aymar, Brandt (ed.), **The Personality of the Cat,** Bonanza Books, New York, 1958

Bryant, Doris, **Doris Bryant's New Cat Book,** Ives Washburn, Inc., New York, 1969

Carr, William H., **The Basic Book of the Cat,** Gramercy Publishing Co., New York, 1968

Denis, Armand, **Cats of the World,** Houghton Mifflin Co., Boston, 1964

Gilbert, John, **Cats, Cats, Cats, Cats,** Paul Hamlyn, London, 1968

Mellen, Ida M., **A Practical Cat Book,** Charles Scribner's Sons, New York, 1950

Mery, Fernand, **The Life, History and Magic of the Cat,** Grosset and Dunlap, New York, 1968

Miller, Harry, **The Common Sense Book of Kitten and Cat Care,** Bantam Books, Inc., New York, 1966

Montgomery, John, **The World of Cats,** Paul Hamlyn, London, 1967

Pond, Grace, **The Observer's Book of Cats,** Frederick Warne and Co., London, 1959

Smith, Richard C., **The Complete Cat Book,** Walker and Company, New York, 1963

Spies, Joseph R., **The Compleat Cat,** Prentice-Hall, New York, 1966

Van Vechten, Carl, **Tiger in the House,** Alfred A. Knopf, New York, 1936

Whitney, Leon F., **Complete Book of Cat Care,** Doubleday, 1953

INDEX

DEF